The Wealthy Divorcee

First published in 2013 by Panoma Press
48 St Vincent Drive, St Albans, Herts, AL1 5SJ, UK

info@panomapress.com
www.panomapress.com

Cover design by Susan Meaney
Book layout by Sophie Norman

Printed on acid-free paper from managed forests. This book
is printed on demand to fulfill orders, so no copies will be
remaindered or pulped.

ISBN 978-1-909623-09-5

The Wealthy DIVORCEE

A step-by-step guide to navigating the finances during and after divorce

HANNAH FOXLEY

Chartered Financial Planner and Fellow of the Personal Finance Society

I would like to dedicate this book to my Dad, the late Bill Foxley. I miss you everyday Dad.

Acknowledgements

Firstly to my friends and family for their support and, in particular, my best friend Tina Jurascheck-Eley for always being there and supporting me without question. You have no idea how grateful I am.

To Salli Glover and the Scarlett community for your amazing support and coaching. You took me from a being a tired and broken woman and gave me wings.

Thank you also to my lovely mentor Vanessa Vallely for your support, encouragement and connecting me to the right people.

To the fantastic Key Person of Influence programme. I would never have written this book otherwise. I have learned so much and you have brought me into the most amazing community of people and for that I am eternally grateful.

To all the wonderful, generous people who I am surrounded by, you know who you are and you are all amazing. I feel blessed to have you all in my life.

To all the people that I have worked with over the years and all of the lessons that you have taught me. They have made me the person that I am today and for that I am truly grateful.

PREFACE

Having worked in the financial services industry for 14 years and often been the only woman in the room at meetings, I understand how under-represented female independent financial advisers are. I have also noticed that women are not comfortable in seeking financial advice because they think that they will be made to feel silly for not having an understanding of financial planning and a grip on the finances. There is a fundamental lack of trust in seeking financial advice and a stereotypical view of a middle aged man in a grey suit, which sadly is not too far from the truth. This does not fill women with confidence or the desire to seek financial advice, so they tend to adopt a head in the sand approach, which is not conducive to a secure future. I want to change that point of view and so my mission is to redefine the way that women feel about seeking financial advice.

Years of speaking to women and exploring the issues they face, particularly when going through divorce has revealed that one of their biggest fears is the finances.

The problem is that as little girls we were told that it is rude to talk about or ask for money. At school, we were not taught basic skills in relation to money and so have grown up with no real idea of how to manage the finances or what financial terminology means. We were taught that it wasn't really our job to look after the money and so were given no skills to do it. However, the whole world has changed since then and in 40% of households in Britain the female is the main breadwinner and with around 45% of marriages ending in divorce, suddenly we are in position where we are managing the money. Even those of us who are used to managing the family finances have an inbuilt fear about money.

For some women, the thought of having to deal with the finances is absolutely terrifying and they have no idea what the household outgoings are, let alone where to start in making decisions about pensions and other assets of the marriage. Other women are comfortable with managing the day-to-day finances and know what the assets of the marriage are but would be daunted by making decisions that ultimately affect their future financial security.

Pensions for example are an incredibly complex and technical area of finance and need specialist advice from a financial planner especially when it comes to deciding on the split in divorce. There is a fundamental lack of understanding of their true value and so they are often not adequately considered as part of the settlement.

In writing this book I have drawn on all of my experience and understanding of the issues that women face in relation to financial planning and managing the finances as well as the information that they need to know and condensed it into a straightforward format that is simple to follow.

The objective of the book is to take the fear and mystery out of finance so that women can confidently make the decisions that need to be made.

Contents

INTRODUCTION

I wanted to start by telling you a bit about me. I have been a financial planner for 10 years and having worked in a male dominated environment, I have always had to be way more qualified to be taken seriously, especially being a young woman in a world of middle aged men. This has served me well though as I studied hard and, as a result, am now both a Chartered Financial Planner and a Fellow of the Personal Finance Society, in fact, I was in the first 1,000 people in the country to achieve this.

Working in a male dominated environment made me very competitive and I picked up some very male characteristics, which I have now realised women found a real turn off. I had lost my identity and my authenticity as a woman.

Even with all of these qualifications and knowledge, I didn't take my own advice and I didn't protect myself financially. I fell into the trap that most of us women do and thought that I was invincible and it would never happen to me. I was young, fit and healthy and had never had a sniff of any sort of illness other than the occasional cold.

In December 2010, I lost my beloved Dad, holding his hand as he took his last breath. He was 87 when he died so he had lived a long life. His name was Bill Foxley and he was an icon in his own right, being described as the worst burnt, surviving airman of the Second World War. He lost his face and most of his hands going back to rescue his comrades from a burning plane. He was the navigator of a Wellington Bomber, which crashed during a training flight. Part of the famous Guinea Pig Club, a group of men who were worked on by the revered plastic surgeon, Archibald McIndoe, and who were guinea pigs for many of the plastic surgery techniques still used today. My Dad became a regular spokesman on the subject and appeared in the famous film The Battle of Britain. He was an icon for positivity and courage in the face of adversity and inspired many others in his lifetime, including me.

Exactly eight months to the day after my dad passed away, I was sitting in the hospital with my best friend being told that I had breast cancer. I was 33 years old. I felt like my whole world had just collapsed around me. I had no family nearby, no partner and no one to help me pay the bills if I got really sick. I had no idea how I was going to get through the gruelling treatment that I faced alone. I was absolutely terrified. Was this going to kill me? What would happen to my horse? What would happen if I couldn't work and pay my bills? Was I going to lose everything? I felt like someone had just pulled the rug out from underneath me. The only relief was that my Dad was not in this world to hear my news, as it would have broken his heart.

So, I started on the conveyor belt of cancer treatment, which included operations to remove the cancer, six months of chemotherapy, followed by daily radiotherapy.

Because I had not protected myself financially, I had to work throughout the treatment so that I could keep the roof over my head. It was hell and I wouldn't wish it on my worst enemy. Chemo literally poisons your body from the inside; it destroys all of your cells and the healthy ones regenerate. Dragging myself out of bed when I felt like I was being killed slowly just to make a cup of tea was hard enough, let alone having to drag myself into the office to work. I had no immune system and was not supposed to be in crowded places, but I had to travel on the train and tube to get to work. A stomach bug would have killed me! By some miracle, I didn't catch anything.

Just as I was getting to the end of chemo and was so low that putting one foot in front of another felt like climbing a mountain, I got a final kick in the kidneys. Against the odds and a very rare occurrence, the cancer had returned. As I drove home from hearing that news, I was planning my demise, mentally checking off Will, selling my horse, what to do with the dogs, life cover in place to pay mortgage (I had ensured that things were taken care of if I died, but hadn't protected myself in case I lived!). I really thought this was the beginning of the end. I didn't think I had any fight left in me.

Being my father's daughter, though, I wasn't going to be beaten. I had a couple of days of crying and despair as I broke the news to my family and friends and then something inside me galvanised and I went into fight mode. It's amazing what looking death in the face does to you and it was the catalyst that has changed my life beyond all recognition, for the better.

I took a real, good, hard look at myself and the person that I had become and I didn't like what I saw. I had been cruising through life being mediocre. I was highly qualified, good at my job and well paid, but I wasn't happy working for someone else. I had no passion in my life, either in a relationship or for what I did. Being stripped back to nothing when losing my hair, eyebrows and eyelashes during chemo, and then being told that they were taking my breast too, made me completely reassess what I felt defined me. I had to look inside to really find myself and I took myself on a transformation process.

I wondered how many women could find themselves in my financial position because they had not protected themselves. I also realised that the majority of my clients were male. Where were the women and who was looking after their needs?

While completing radiotherapy, I started to network and speak to other women. I asked them what they wanted and why they didn't seek financial advice. The overwhelming response was that, as women, we don't feel confident around money, no matter how experienced or otherwise we are in dealing with the finances. We don't want to speak to a crusty, middle aged IFA, or a younger sleazy guy (sorry, boys, not my words!). The sad fact is that many women have no financial protection and a general head in the sand approach to money. I decided that I wanted to change that.

Ten days after finishing radiotherapy, I quit my job and started my business. I was absolutely terrified, but also excited as well. I just knew that I had to follow my heart, feel the fear and do it anyway.

That has been the theme of my life ever since. I feel that the old me died the day that I was told the cancer came back and a new me was born. I have lived permanently outside of my comfort zone ever since and I have had breakthrough after breakthrough. I feel like a different person and my purpose in life is to educate and support women, both as an inspiration by showing how much positive can come from something so negative and also so that they can become more confident around money.

My mission is to redefine the way women feel about financial planning; I am known for transforming women's futures and I leave them feeling confident, secure and liberated.

Why have I told you all this? I wanted you to know that I understand the emotions that you are facing right now; fear, terror and uncertainty, like your world has just collapsed. I have, therefore, brought to the book that empathy and understanding of your emotions. I hope that I can also give you some inspiration that if you can keep pushing through this hell, on the other side is sunlight.

I have written this book to help you through one of the scariest parts of the divorce process, the finances. I have tried to consider all situations in the writing of this book, from the woman who has no financial knowledge at all, to the woman who is used to dealing with the finances but doesn't have the technical knowledge to understand the finances in divorce. Some of the information is therefore, very basic, and some of it is far more advanced. I have also assumed that you have been married for some time and are entitled to a good share of your husband's assets.

I have taken all of my years of experience as a Chartered Financial Planner and used them to create you a step-by-step guide to navigating the minefield that is dealing with the finances on divorce and after. It will help you with everything from opening a bank account to budgeting, to buying a house, to investing and understanding debt. It will be your guide and your friend and you can dip in and out of it whenever you need to. The more times you read it, the more you will see and learn.

It will help you to avoid making the common financial mistakes that many women make when getting divorced. By understanding what the pitfalls are and the ways to avoid them and confront them, you will be able to make more informed decisions that will have a positive impact on your future financial security.

In order that I can address all of the potential financial issues that you may encounter when going through a divorce, I have had to take a more negative view of the man you are divorcing. I appreciate that not all men are devious and unfair, but unfortunately, some are. I have, therefore, had to write the book from the angle of the worst-case scenario when discussing the issues that you may face.

Keep this book close to you so that you can refer to it whenever you need to. Absorb the information within it and let it guide you through this difficult time. Do the exercises within it and don't be afraid to write in it and make notes.

I hope that you find it useful. I very much enjoyed writing it for you.

CHAPTER 1

Common financial mistakes made in a divorce

I think the best place to start is to look at the common financial mistakes made when going through a divorce. The aim of this book is to help you gain a better understanding of the finance issues in a divorce and to understand the finances better in general so that you can continue your life without fearing them. The key is to be strategic about it and take emotion out of the decisions that you make. This is easier said than done, I know. You may be feeling anger, sadness, loss, fear and probably terror at the thought of what the future holds. However, making financial decisions with your heart and not your head is absolutely fatal. The decisions that you make now will affect you for the rest of your life and you must, therefore, treat this like a business transaction. This is why it is so important to have people around you who can help you to be objective about the decisions you make.

Here is my list of the common financial mistakes that are made when going through a divorce.

1. Failing to identify debt and credit file issues

Not understanding what is lurking on your credit file can

be a massive mistake. Many women can find that there has been credit taken out in their name that they had no idea about. There could be missed payments and defaults that you were not aware of, which will stop you getting credit of your own. Chapter 2 discusses this in more detail.

2. Thinking that you need to pay for the most expensive lawyer that money can buy

It is, of course, important to find a good lawyer, but you do not have to find the most expensive one. Good lawyers aren't always the most expensive, they are the ones with the good experience and track record. Remember, the more you spend on legal fees, the less money there will be for you both in the settlement. Chapter 2 discusses this in more detail.

3. Failing to consider other dispute resolution options such as mediation and collaboration

A divorce does not necessarily have to mean a bloody dispute that gets dragged through the courts. If it is possible to settle things in a more agreeable way, there are other options that may be more suitable and less costly. Chapter 2 explains these in more detail for you.

4. Failing to understand the roles of different professionals in a divorce

Your lawyer is there to advise you on the legal aspects of the divorce and help you to get the right settlement. They are not a financial adviser or a counsellor and are unable to advise in either of these areas. Hours spent on the phone to them talking through the emotional side of things is going to cost you a fortune; they are a very expensive friend.

Likewise, asking them to help you with budgeting and financial planning is fruitless as they are unable to advise in these areas. Chapter 2 walks you through using the right professional for the job and the role of a financial planner.

5. **Dealing with financial assets on a single basis rather than taking account of the bigger picture**

   Looking at dividing every single asset of the marriage in isolation and dividing each asset individually is a big mistake. You need to take a big picture view of all of the assets and how they interact with each other. A financial planner can help you to do this. Chapter 2 explains the role of a financial planner in the divorce process.

6. **Bringing emotional attachment to the financial assets and not thinking strategically**

   The biggest mistake that you can make is to make emotional decisions. Emotional decisions are not rational ones and when it comes to money you absolutely must make strategic and rational decisions. This is, of course, easier said than done. Chapter 2 talks about why you must detach yourself and the role of a divorce coach in the process.

7. **Keeping a house that you can't afford**

   One of the biggest mistakes in a divorce is hanging on to the marital home because of an emotional attachment to it. This can be both emotionally and financially destructive. If you end up giving up everything else in lieu of keeping the house, this can have a devastating impact on your future financial security. Chapter 8 talks about property and walks you through the process of purchasing a new property.

8. Failing to break all financial ties

Once you have made the decision to separate and divorce, you must cut all financial ties as quickly as possible. Keeping joint loans and credit cards can put you in serious hot water as you are both responsible for the whole debt. Likewise, you should close any joint savings accounts and split the assets. Chapter 2 covers this in more detail.

9. Not having a true understanding of the financial assets and debts of the marriage

This can be the biggest downfall of women in a divorce. It is absolutely essential to understand what the assets of the marriage are, as well as the debts. Don't get caught out by finding there are debts that you knew nothing about. If your husband is likely to try and hide assets, which sadly even the most honest of men can try and do, you need to know how to address this. Chapter 2 and chapter 4 discuss this in more detail.

10. Failing to understand what your true outgoings are and preparing an incorrect budget

The form E is the lynchpin of the financial matters in divorce and your outgoings and budget will form the basis of the divorce settlement. If you get this wrong it can affect the rest of your life. Chapter 2 discusses the form E and chapter 3 discusses budgeting in detail.

11. Not understanding your liability for unsecured debt

If you have joint debt, you are both liable for the whole debt, no matter who spent the money. It is important that all unsecured debt is repaid before the divorce completes or you could be left liable for a debt if your ex-husband defaults. More of this in chapters 2 and 4.

12. Assuming that an equal division is a fair division on divorce

Many women fall into the trap of thinking that an equal split of assets is a fair split and because they want to get it over and done with they agree. This can be a big mistake as it's unlikely that that you will have equal earning capacity in the future. Even if you had a high earning job before you were married, if you have taken time out to have a family or you stopped work once you were married, you will not be able to walk straight back into a high paying job. Therefore, settling for an equal split may not be appropriate. It is important to get advice from your lawyer.

13. Failing to understand the risk and reward trade off when offsetting assets

The most common example of this is letting him keep the pension in return for you keeping the family home. Chapter 5 covers pensions in detail and chapter 7 describes the different assets and the risk reward trade off to consider.

14. Having an unrealistic expectation of your lifestyle after divorce

You may not be able to continue with the same lifestyle after divorce. You may have to come to terms with not being able to spend the same amounts of money on the children or go out for dinner with your friends whenever you want. Chapter 3 will help you to learn how to budget effectively and create a spending plan.

15. Failing to understand the true value of your husbands defined benefit pension

This is also known as a final salary scheme and is a pot of gold. If you offset based on the transfer value given in the Form E, it could have a detrimental effect on your future financial security. Chapter 5 explains this to you.

16. Failing to take your fair share of your husband's pensions

An equal split of your husband's pensions is unlikely to be an equitable split if you have been looking after the children and do not have the earning capacity to create a bigger fund in the future. The split needs to be based on equalising your incomes in retirement rather than equalising the split of the current pension pot. Again, this is explained in chapter 5.

17. Taking the house in lieu of the pension

This could be the biggest financial mistake that you make and yet so many people do it. A house that you live in has no future income value, but it has costs associated with it and you cannot remove bricks to take to the supermarket to buy your shopping when you have retired.

18. Not taking into consideration the impact of tax on assets

Taxation can have a huge impact on the division of assets as well as your future cash flow, and failing to take account of this can have a devastating effect on your asset position and future financial security. Chapter 11 explains the basics of tax to you.

19. Failing to change joint insurance policies

Once you have made the decision to separate, it is vital that you change any insurance policies into your own name. If you were to die, the proceeds of a joint policy would go to your ex-husband and he is also likely to be the beneficiary of any trusts you have set up. This may not be appropriate going forward and so needs to be considered. Chapter 6 explains the different protection policies and why you need them.

20. Failing to make a new Will

Your Will is almost certain to either be a mirror Will (which means that you and your husband's Wills are identical, leaving everything to each other) or leave everything to your husband. You need to change this as soon as you separate as it would be disastrous if you died and all of your assets went to your ex-husband rather than your children, family, friends or chosen charities if this was not what you wanted. Chapter 2 explains this in more detail.

21. Failing to insure the maintenance payments and maintain control of the policies

Once maintenance payments have been agreed, it is essential to get cover in place to protect them in the event of death or illness of your husband. Furthermore, you must be the person in control of these policies so that you know if he defaults on paying them, thereby cancelling the policies. This is covered in detail in chapter 6.

22. Not understanding the liquidity of assets

It is vital to understand the liquidity of assets that you are being offered as part of the divorce settlement so that you do not accept something that you will not later be able to turn to cash. Chapter 7 explains different assets and the risks of them in terms of being able to turn them into cash.

23. Failing to consider your long-term security

Only looking at the current value of assets rather than considering the long-term value can have a devastating effect on your future financial security. For example, taking a car in lieu of a cash asset or an ISA portfolio is just crazy. You have just accepted a depreciating asset over an asset that can and will increase in value. The house versus the pension falls within this category also. This is why a financial adviser is key.

24. Forgetting about the long-term impact of inflation, tax and having an unrealistic expectation of investment returns

Inflation has a huge impact on the future value of money and failing to take it into consideration when calculating future cash flows will mean that your money will not last. Tax also erodes income and assets and so it must be considered in calculations. An unrealistic expectation of future returns will mean that you will run out of money! A good financial planner is essential. Chapters 2, 10 and 11 will help explain this.

25. Failing to develop a post-divorce financial plan

You absolutely must have financial advice during and after your divorce. Failing to properly plan your future financial security could mean a very poor lifestyle in later life. You need to ensure that you have adequate protection in place and that you plan for later life rather than just focussing on the now. A financial planner who uses proper cash flow analysis software will do this for you.

CHAPTER 2

Where do I start?
The things you absolutely have to do

In this chapter I will take you through the essential areas that you need to act on quickly to ensure that you don't get caught out in the early stages. No matter how amicable things are at the start, money and desperation can have a terrible effect on someone and turn them into an irrational being. The best thing that you can do is to be very strategic about things and not let emotions cloud your judgement when it comes to getting the money side sorted out.

Detach yourself emotionally from the money issues

This I appreciate is easier said than done as you will have great emotional attachment to things like the marital home. However, decisions based on emotions are never good ones and you don't want to spend the rest of your life regretting making rash decisions because you let your emotions rule. You need to be extremely strategic when it comes to the money side and look at it as a cold business transaction. Do not try and use money to punish your husband for your pain, it will not have a good outcome. I will speak later in the chapter about the value of a divorce coach to help you come to terms with the emotional side of the divorce, which will help you to be more rational in your thinking when it comes to the money side. Bad decisions about money now could cost you dear for the rest of your life.

Get a grip on money

The most important thing you need to do once it has become clear that divorce is the only option and you have separated is to get a grip on the money side of things. Yes, it may sound cold and calculating, but a bit of work now will save you a lot of pain and possible cost in the future. Money makes people behave very irrationally and even if things are amicable now, when it comes to giving up money, men can behave very badly. They may try and hide assets so that they don't have to share them with you. Not all men are like this and some are very rational and reasonable, I am painting a worst-case scenario picture here so that you are prepared for all eventualities. If your husband has complex financial affairs and a business, there is greater scope for him to hide assets. As I have said, this will feel very cold and calculating, but you have to treat it as a business transaction and ensure that you get what you are rightly entitled to. You will have to live on this money for the rest of your life, particularly if you do not have the ability to earn a large salary, so you need to ensure that you don't get cheated out of assets that you have a right to.

Get copies of paperwork

It is a good idea to start to gather this information before it gets to the point of agreeing to separate in case your husband decides to try and hide things as soon as the decision has been made. You will need to look for bank statements, credit card statements, mortgage statements, pension statements, share certificates, land registry documents, annual statements from investments, contract notes for shares and investments, tax returns, company accounts, savings certificates or statements, policy documents for life cover, critical illness cover, income protection and private medical cover and trust documentation. This will seem like a very daunting prospect but you need copies of everything and you need to keep the copies in a safe place, which is not your home. You could leave them with a member of your own family or a friend who is not a joint friend and who you can absolutely trust. If you have any doubts at all then get yourself a safety deposit box. If you look it up on Google, there are lots of places that come up in London and around the country.

You may need professional help to get the information that you require and I will discuss this later in the chapter.

You may have to get a court order to freeze assets if your husband is likely to start trying to hide money or move it to jurisdictions that do not have to recognise UK law. The proviso here is that you can legally only take copies of papers that are in either yours or joint names and a lawyer cannot accept copies of papers that are not in your name. So, if you find assets that are in his name only, make a note of what they are and the policy number but leave the paperwork.

Break all financial ties

Once you have made a decision to separate, you need to close all joint accounts, especially joint loans and credit cards, as quickly as you can. I appreciate that it may not be possible to do this immediately if you have mortgage payments coming out of a joint account.

It is unwise to accept him saying that he will pay off the loans and credit cards and then trusting him to do it. You are both liable for the full amount of borrowing on a joint account so he could run up massive debt and default on it meaning that the creditors come after you for it all. I will talk about getting a credit file and what it tells you later in the chapter but you must be absolutely vigilant with this.

Joint savings accounts can be emptied by your husband, leaving you with nothing, so agree on a split and get your share of the money out of the joint accounts and close the accounts.

You also need to change joint life policies into single names and make a new Will. You do not want your (soon to be) ex-husband benefitting from your life policies and assets once you have separated if you do not feel this would be appropriate. I will explain this in more detail later in the chapter.

Opening a bank account

If you are quite used to managing your own money and have your own accounts you can ignore this section.

However, if all of your accounts are in joint names and you are not used to managing your own money, this section will walk you through how to do it.

Before you can move money from a joint account you will need to open one in your own name. The process is fairly simple and there are several ways that you can go about it depending on how comfortable you are with technology and using the Internet.

Opening an account online:

The process of opening a bank account online these days is very simple and is my preferred method, mainly because I hate having to go into the bank and waiting around for someone to see me.

If you are comfortable with doing the process online, the first port of call is www.moneysupermarket.com, which is a comparison website that will give you comparisons of pretty much anything you can think of. For the purposes of this, though, you will need to go into the money section and click on bank accounts.

You will need to decide if you are happy to do most of your transactions online or over the phone or whether you will prefer to speak with someone face to face in a branch.

If you are happy to do most of your banking online or over the phone, then I think First Direct give a great service, and if you need to call them for something, you get to speak to a real person rather than having to go through a million and one options, only to have to deal with an automated system, which is incredibly frustrating.

Don't get sucked into the accounts that offer you free insurances in return for a monthly fee, as you can usually buy the individual insurances more cheaply than buying them as a package through a bank account.

Once you have chosen a bank account through the money supermarket portal, follow the link to the provider's website and go through the application. The beauty of doing it all online is that the bank can do all of its security checks electronically and you don't have to take your passport and proof of address to the bank separately.

The application will take you through a credit check and will ask you questions about your income, outgoings, employment (if any), whether you are a home owner and what other bank accounts or credit cards you have. Once you have answered these, you will then get a decision from the bank. This will either be an instant yes, an instant no or, alternatively, it will be referred to the bank to be looked at more closely.

If you are given the option, I would opt for online statements rather than statements through the post as they can't be opened by someone else. This means that you can have some privacy.

Assuming that you get an instant yes, you will then be given an application number and possibly an immediate sort code and account number and told what the next steps are. A confirmation email will be sent to your email address. As soon as you receive your sort code and account number, you can transfer money to the account. You will then receive your bank card and a cheque book if you have requested one.

Branch based accounts:

You can pop into a local branch and open an account in person if you are not comfortable with the online process. My advice would be not to open your own account at the same bank and branch as you hold your joint accounts. Yes, you are protected by the Data Protection Act, but if your husband is also known to the branch, it only takes a friendly member of bank staff to say to your husband: 'I saw your wife here the other day', without realising the potential impact and it could cause problems for you.

You will need to take some identification with you if you are going to open a bank account in person. This will be either a passport or driving licence and proof of address, which can be a utility bill, credit card bill or bank statement dated within the last three months. You can also take your passport and then use your driving licence to verify your address.

You will be taken through the same process as online; you will need to know income, outgoings, employment details (if any), other bank accounts and credit cards that you have.

Again, you will be given either an instant yes, instant no or a referral for a decision.

Once you have a bank account open in your own name, you will be able to transfer money into it from the joint account.

A word on email accounts

If your husband knows your email address and is likely to know your password, set up a new email address. It is very simple to set up a hotmail, yahoo or gmail email account. Make the email address something a little less obvious and use a password that your husband won't guess. Also remember that email is not a secure method of communication and emails can easily be read, if someone is intent on finding out what is in your emails.

Get crystal clear on your debt and credit file position

It is a sad fact that some women are blissfully unaware that their husbands have been obtaining credit in their name for all sorts of things. This is bad enough, but if he has not been maintaining the payments on this credit then you are not going to be able to obtain any because your credit history is bad. You need to be absolutely clear about what is on your credit file and so you need to get a copy of yours.

Checking your credit file

Your credit file is a record of all of the credit that has ever been obtained in your name, as well as any financial associations that have been made with you, and it is a very telling document.

Those of us who work in the financial services industry are very familiar with them, as we have to provide them to the regulator regularly. Many people who are not familiar with the financial services industry are not aware of their existence, particularly those who have not had a lot of credit in the past.

This document will tell you whether your husband has obtained credit in your name without you realising and it will also show if you have been financially associated with another person without your knowledge. It is not unusual for women to find mortgages for properties that they had no idea of, or credit cards and loans taken in their name that they were not aware of. On a less sinister note, it will show you what credit you have taken out before, if you have missed any payments and how credit worthy you are, which is vital to know if you are going to be in charge of your own financial situation. It is an essential document to have and be aware of.

Whenever you apply for credit (which includes a bank account or a mobile phone contract), the lender will contact the credit agencies electronically and perform a search. The information on your file will tell the lender how much risk you pose to them financially. I will cover debt in more detail in chapter 4, but the things that will affect your credit worthiness are how much credit you have available to you, any missed payments, any defaults (where consistent payments have been missed) and how much credit you are currently using. So, for example, if you had available credit to you of £10,000 and you are constantly in debt of £9,000 that is likely to have a negative effect.

There are three main credit agencies that hold this information and provide it to the lenders, and these are Equifax, Experian and Call Credit. Experian and Equifax are the most commonly used credit reference agencies.

You can obtain a statutory credit report from any of them for £2 and this will give you a complete picture of your credit file. Get this and keep it safe along with the other documents that you have been collecting.

When you go online to get this through Experian or Equifax, they will try and sell you their credit check report product. In the long term you won't need this product but it could be very useful in the short term, as it will send you alerts when changes to your credit file occur, such as new credit being obtained. It costs £14.99 a month to have credit alerts sent to you. If your husband tries to take out credit in your name or there are any defaults or missed payments to credit that you have, you will know sooner rather than later.

Get absolutely clear about your costs and budget

One of the most common financial mistakes in a divorce is failing to produce an accurate budget for the Form E and, therefore, the settlement. I will describe the Form E later in the chapter, and Chapter 3 describes in detail how to create a budget and spending plan, both for the divorce and for your living requirements once the settlement has been agreed. You need to think about EVERYTHING you spend money on. You will also have to accept that your standard of living may need to change post separation and divorce as you will only have a finite amount of money.

The professionals that you will need

Having the right professionals for the job is essential and will save you money in the long run. Your lawyer is there to help you through the legal process. They are not a relationship coach, private investigator or financial planner. This section explains all of the professionals that you may need as part of the financial side of the divorce. You may also need others to help you with the children but it is not my area of expertise and so I shall stick with what I know.

Through my work I have met and know all the professionals that I have listed below. I would be delighted to put you in touch with anyone that you need. A Google search will lead you to me very easily.

The Family Lawyer

The role of the lawyer is to help you through the legal aspects of the divorce as well as to help you to secure a fair and proper financial settlement. They may also be involved in the agreement over the contact rights for the children if there is a dispute and you instruct them to do so.

You will need a good, experienced divorce lawyer who is well used to negotiating financial settlements. If your finances are complex you will need a financial specialist lawyer. I will explain the different ways of resolving the divorce in a moment.

Do not fall into the trap of thinking that you need to find the most expensive lawyer to handle your divorce.

Do your research and make a strategic and not an emotional decision. Start by asking any friends, family or acquaintances that have been through divorce for a recommendation. Make sure that their experience was positive and that they felt that they got a good outcome. This is, of course, very difficult to quantify.

You will have your own preference as to whether you want to deal with a man or a woman, but you may feel more comfortable with a woman if you have had a difficult time with your husband.

When choosing a lawyer, don't be afraid to ask about their experience and what sorts of cases they have dealt with previously; question the outcomes that they have had on their cases. If you are dealing with a complex financial situation, it is essential that you have a lawyer that is used to dealing with this.

There are several different ways to deal with the divorce process and, ultimately, the route you choose will depend on how contentious the divorce is and how complex the financial situation is. The Resolution website is a great source of information and tips to help you with the divorce and separation process and I recommend that you have a look. www.resolution.org.uk. The following are the four main methods for the divorce process in the UK.

Arbitration

This is an alternative method to going to court. You will agree between you to appoint an arbitrator to make a decision on the property and financial issues. An arbitrator is an independent party whose decision is final and binding once made. You, therefore, have to be comfortable that your finances can be decided in this more simplistic way. If your financial affairs are complex or there is a risk that your partner may hide assets, this route is unlikely to be suitable.

The same person will deal with all issues that arise and you and your partner will have a say in how the proceedings are run. You can ask the arbitrator to deal with all of the financial issues, or just one or two issues that have arisen.

This solution has been designed to be much faster, more flexible and more cost-effective than going to court. It is also confidential.

Mediation

What is mediation?
Mediators are trained to help resolve disputes over all issues faced by separating couples, or specific issues such as arrangements for any children. A mediator will meet with you and your partner together and will identify those issues you can't agree on and help you to try and reach agreement.

Mediators are neutral and will not take sides, so they cannot give advice to either of you. They will usually recommend that you obtain legal advice alongside the mediation process and will guide you as to when this should happen. However, Resolution's trained lawyer mediators will provide general legal information to both of you within the mediation if this is appropriate. Some are qualified to consult with children in mediation.

How does mediation work?
You may contact a mediator directly or your solicitor may refer you. What can you expect to happen?

Mediation assessment

Not everyone is ready for mediation at the same stage in separating, so the mediator needs to find out whether it is suitable for both of you.

Since April 2011, there has been a requirement (with some exceptions) that anybody wanting to go to court should attend a meeting (called a MIAM) with an appropriately qualified mediator to find out about mediation and other non-court options.

Publically funded mediators will also assess your eligibility for financial assistance and explain charges if you are not eligible. If you ultimately decide not to mediate, this stage is necessary if you want to go to court, as the court will expect a certificate from the mediator before you start proceedings to show that you tried it.

The mediator will speak to you briefly about the process to ensure you understand how it works. They will then contact your partner and have the same conversation with them. Sometimes mediators prefer to do this face to face rather than on the telephone.

Working out the details:

- Further meetings will be scheduled at which you may work on communication issues, renew arrangements for children, exchange financial information and consider options. The mediator may suggest other help, such as financial advice or support for your children. Between meetings you may wish to meet with your lawyer for advice.

Finalising the proposals:

- Once you have proposals you both find acceptable, the mediator will prepare a summary of them together with a summary of the financial information, which will be sent to each of you to discuss with your lawyers. After you have both received legal advice, and if you are both still happy with the proposals, the lawyers will convert the summary into a legally binding document and oversee any necessary implementation.

Source: www.resolution.org.uk

Collaboration

Collaboration is a fairly new concept in the UK and I have used the Wikipedia definition here to describe it.

Collaborative law (also called collaborative practice, divorce, or family law) is a legal process enabling couples who have decided to separate or end their marriage to work with their lawyers and, on occasion, other family professionals in order to avoid the uncertain outcome of court and to achieve a settlement that best meets the specific needs of both parties and their children without the underlying threat of contested litigation. The voluntary process is initiated when the couple signs a contract (called the "participation agreement"), binding each other to the process and disqualifying their respective lawyer's right to represent either one in any future family related litigation.

The collaborative process can be used to facilitate a broad range of other family issues, including disputes between parents and the drawing up of pre and post-marital contracts. The traditional method of drawing up pre-marital contracts is oppositional, and many couples prefer to begin their married life on a better footing where documents are drawn up consensually and together.

It can still be fairly expensive as you each need your own lawyer and it is advisable to have a financial planner specialising in pensions to advise you on the finances. If you are unable to reach an agreement using this process and you decide to go to court, the lawyer that you have used for the collaboration process will not be able to represent you.

Full court proceedings

This is likely to be the most expensive and lengthy way to get divorced. You will each need a solicitor to act for you and the judge will make the final decision as to the financial split and contact rights for the children if this is an issue. The judges have quite a wide discretion, and whilst they have to make decisions within the law, the discretion they have means that you could get a different outcome on a different day depending on the judge. The court process can bring much uncertainty. If the divorce is contested, or there are issues with the children or your husband is being very difficult over the finances, it could take years to reach a settlement and, in the process, a huge amount of money. Where things are very difficult between you or there are significant financial assets to consider, this is likely to be the only option.

The Private Investigator

Hiring a private investigator may sound a bit James Bond but if you suspect that your husband is hiding assets, particularly overseas, you are likely to need one. If you are divorcing a particularly wealthy husband, it is highly likely that a private investigator or some sort of surveillance could be involved on both sides. It is also likely to be faster and cheaper than lawyers fighting it out between themselves and getting nowhere. The cost will depend on the amount of work required to dig out the information. Again, remember to be strategic and business like in this approach don't get emotionally involved. You need to find out what assets he has so that you can ensure a fair settlement. The information that you gain may or may not be able to be used in court, but knowledge is power and it can help you in negotiations to know exactly what the situation is.

The Divorce Coach

I am a huge advocate of coaching and have a coach myself. She has literally changed my life by helping me to change my whole way of thinking.

The emotional side of the divorce can eat away at you and make you feel really bitter. This is not good for your health, your finances or for your children. A coach will help you come to terms with what is happening and help you to move on more quickly and deal with emotions and feelings that are not serving you.

Having a clearer mind will help you deal with the divorce in the business-like manner that it needs to be dealt with to get you the best outcome.

Actuary

An actuary is a professional who specialises in complex financial calculations and, in this case, it will be for pension analysis. They are essentially an expert in number crunching. If your husband has a final salary pension scheme, the figure that the employer sends as a transfer value is quite often wrong and bears no relevance to the true future value of that pension. It is, therefore, vital to get an actuarial calculation of that future value to ensure that you get your fair share. Actuarial calculations reveal the true value of that pension, which can then be used in your negotiations. It will be difficult, if not impossible, to split it accurately without this information, especially if your husband is some way from retirement or there is a significant age gap between you.

Forensic Accountant

If your husband has his own business, you may need a forensic accountant to look at the accounts and value the business. They are a specialist practice area of accounting who get involved in disputes, litigation and fraud and their evidence is suitable for use in court, hence the term 'forensic'. For this reason, they are certainly not cheap. You and your husband can instruct the same accountant to act independently for both of you and he will prepare evidence for the court, or if the court agrees, you can each instruct your own independent accountant. If you instruct one to work on both sides initially, you will not then be able to instruct the same accountant to work for either side if there is still dispute.

The Financial Planner

A good financial planner is an essential part of the divorce process, both during and after. A mistake that is often made is involving the financial planner at the end once the settlement has been agreed, but they can add much value in helping to reach a settlement.

Some of the mistakes mentioned in chapter 1 can be avoided by having a financial planner involved at the beginning of the process.

A good financial planner will bring to your attention and help you avoid making the following mistakes, which we identified in the first chapter;

- Dealing with financial assets on a single basis rather than taking account of the bigger picture
- Keeping a house that you can't afford
- Failing to break all financial ties
- Not having a true understanding of the financial assets and debts of a marriage
- Failing to understand what your true outgoings are and preparing an incorrect budget
- Assuming that an equal division is a fair division on divorce
- Failing to understand the risk and reward trade off when offsetting assets
- Having an unrealistic expectation of your lifestyle after divorce
- Failing to understand the true value of your husband's defined benefit pension scheme
- Failing to take your fair share of your husband's pensions
- Taking the house in lieu of the pension
- Not taking into consideration the impact of tax on assets
- Failing to change joint life policies
- Failing to insure the maintenance payments and maintain control of policies
- Not understanding the liquidity of assets
- Failing to consider your long-term security
- Forgetting about the long-term impact of inflation and tax and having unrealistic expectations of investment returns
- Failing to develop a post-divorce financial plan

So, as you can see, having a financial planner is key.
Here are some of the ways that they can help you.

Help you with preparing the Form E

The Form E is the financial statement document in a divorce and is the lynchpin of the financial decision-making. It is absolutely vital to get the information on it correct. The most crucial part for you to get right is part 3, which relates to the financial requirements that you have both in terms of capital and income. This is where any mistakes in the budget could have a negative impact on the settlement that you agree. It is imperative to include absolutely everything on that statement and take into account the impact of inflation and tax.

In addition to that, a financial adviser can help you to fill out the rest the form by assisting you to obtain all of the relevant information about your savings, investments and pensions from the providers. Because they see this paperwork all of the time, they know exactly what they are looking for and can take the stress away from you and save your solicitor time also.

It will also be vital to cross reference what your husband puts on the Form E with the information that you have gathered yourself and, if required, from the private detective to find any discrepancies in what he has disclosed. They can help you with this too.

Understanding the assets

If your husband has many different assets and investments, you will need to understand exactly what they are, how risky they are, what the tax implications are and whether you can actually sell them. You will also need to understand the future value of those investments and how they will help your future financial security rather than focussing on the current value of it. Your husband is likely to have a different risk profile to you and so you will need someone who really understands the assets to explain them to you. A financial planner can do this for you.

Getting to grips with the pensions

Getting your share of your husband's pension is absolutely crucial and it's not just about agreeing an equal split based on the current value of the funds, doing this could be seriously detrimental to you. There are many factors to consider when looking at splitting the pension and they are a significant asset in most marriages, so getting it right is crucial. Only a financial adviser can advise on pensions. They work with the lawyer and the actuary, if a final salary pension scheme is involved to bring the figures to life and explain the impact of the factors used in the calculations. I will discuss this in greater detail in the chapter 4.

Calculating your future income needs

When calculating your future income needs factors such as inflation, tax and investment returns need to be taken into consideration so that you do not run out of money. Failure to take these factors into consideration can and will have a devastating effect on your future financial security.

A good financial planner uses specialist software, which can analyse future cash flow requirements taking into account inflation, tax and different investment returns to calculate the sum that would be required as a settlement. This software gives you a visual representation of how different factors can affect your future financial security. It will show when you will run out of money, which allows the financial planner and lawyer to calculate how much of a lump sum you need as a settlement or how much maintenance needs to be paid. It is also used to show how much of your husband's pension you will need to take to ensure that you have a fair income in retirement. It clearly shows the effects of inflation and investment returns on your money and is brilliant for helping you to plan and budget. The results of this analysis and the assumptions used can be used to produce a report to provide to the court. The planner will then use this software for the post-divorce financial planning to help you set a realistic budget to live on so that you don't run out of money. This is the true value of a great financial planner.

Protection of the settlement

You may agree as part of the settlement that your husband will pay you maintenance either until the children reach a certain age, or it may be for the rest of your life. It is essential that this is protected in case your husband becomes sick or dies. It is also vital to ensure that the protection is set up in such a way that you know that he is paying the premiums, and you don't find out when it is too late that he cancelled the policy without you knowing.

I will talk about this in much more depth in the chapter on protection.

Post-divorce financial planning

Once the divorce has been finalised and you have your settlement, you will be on your own financially. Proper financial planning is really important as you don't want to get ten years down the line and run out of money, or get to retirement and realise that you don't have enough.

As described above, financial planners can help you to budget correctly, so that you have money for now and money for the future. You will also need help with school and university fees for the children.

You may have got some of your husband's pension as part of the settlement and this will need to be invested for you, as well as a discussion around adding to it yourself. You may have cash and assets that you have no idea what to do with. This is a very scary and fearful position to be in when you are not used to it and this is where the planner can help. The relationship with your financial planner is a long one and will guide you through life's changes as well as any curve balls that it throws at you.

Choosing the right adviser

All financial advisers must be diploma qualified in order to give financial advice, but as with all professions, knowledge and experience varies between individuals. An adviser who is either Chartered or Certified will have had to complete far more rigorous qualifications as well as having a proven track record in the industry and signing up to a code of ethical conduct.

An independent financial adviser is an agent of you and will give you impartial advice as they are not tied to any company or provider. You will be charged a fee for the advice that they give you. Make sure you really question your adviser to ensure that they are genuinely independent and do not be blinded by fancy literature and marketing material. Your financial planner should use cash flow modelling software to really ensure that they help your lawyer get you the best settlement and to help you plan after the divorce. It is not possible to get a really accurate picture without it and this is where they will really add value to you.

It is important that you trust and feel comfortable with your adviser and that you are able to understand the advice that they have given you. You will have a long-term relationship with them and they will be looking after your financial security.

Change Life Policies and Trust Beneficiaries

Once you have separated you need to check all of your life policies and the trust documentation attached to them. You will need to replace any joint life policies with individual ones. If you were to die and you have a joint life policy, all of the proceeds would be paid to your husband, which is possibly not what you would wish to happen. If you have policies in your own name, you will need to check the trust documentation as it's likely that everything has been left to your husband, or if it's a discretionary trust, he is likely to be the trustee and discretionary beneficiary. I will explain trusts in greater detail in chapter 6. Many people forget to check their life insurance policies when they separate, but they would not want their ex-spouse to benefit from the proceeds.

You may also have benefitted from your husband's private medical cover and will lose the benefit of this once you are divorced. You will need to set up your own policy.

Your financial adviser will be able to advise on this and help you set up new policies in your own name.

Make a Will and a Lasting Power of Attorney

Once you have decided to separate, the first thing you need to do is make a new Will. This is vital if you have children. You should also have a Lasting Power of Attorney (LPA) put in place. They are not the cheeriest of subjects but are so important, and once they are done, you can have peace of mind in knowing that things are taken care of.

What is a Will?

A Will is a document that expresses your wishes about what you would like to happen to your affairs after your death.

You can specify what you want to happen to your financial assets, property, any pets you have and also make arrangements for the care of your children. You can set up trusts within a Will also, which can be for inheritance tax planning and also so that there can be some control over what happens to your assets. For example, you may want your assets to go into a trust for the children rather than them having direct access to the money.

You can make provision for the people that you want to manage your affairs after your death, known as executors. You can also appoint trustees to manage the trusts that you set up within the Will.

A Will is, however, a public document that can be read by anyone after your death and it can also be contested, so if there are likely to be family issues, it is best to set up trusts in your lifetime. A lawyer can advise you on this and it you should have a Will drawn up properly by a lawyer and not use a do-it-yourself pack.

Why do I need a Will?

If you do not have a Will, the law, rather than you or your family, will decide what happens to your affairs. If you die without a Will, you are considered to have died Intestate and the rules of Intestacy apply. The rules of Intestacy do not make any provision for unmarried couples, step-children, friends or charities.

Intestacy rules apply to your financial affairs, but what about the children? It is important that you ensure provision has been made for your children in the event of your death. A lawyer will be able to advise you as to how to go about this to ensure that your wishes are met.

Lasting Power of Attorney (LPA)

What is a Lasting Power of Attorney?

An LPA gives someone permission to act on your behalf if you no longer have the mental capacity to make your own decisions. If you do not have one in place and you lose capacity, either through a health issue or an accident, the court of protection will become involved, which is not a nice process. A family member will have to apply to the court for permission to be appointed as a 'Deputy'. A Deputy is similar to an Attorney, except they are appointed by, and are responsible to, the court, reporting to the court on an annual basis. This is a significantly more expensive and painful process, which can be avoided by having the LPA in place.

There are two types of LPA and you should have each of them:

Health and Welfare:

This gives the attorney the power to make decisions about your health and welfare and includes things such as what medical attention and medication you receive, moving you into a care home and refusing life-sustaining treatment. You need to give very careful consideration to whom you give the power to make these decisions. They must have the same outlook as you, particularly when it comes to your view of life-sustaining treatment. This must be someone who you trust literally with your life.

Property and financial affairs:

This gives the attorney the power to make financial decisions on your behalf. They would be able to pay your bills, collect your benefits and sell your home on your behalf if this needed to be done because you had gone into care. This will make it far simpler for someone to manage your affairs if the need arose.

Choosing an Attorney

Choosing an Attorney is an incredibly important decision and must be someone that you trust implicitly as they will have full control over making decisions about your health and welfare or financial affairs if you are no longer able to make them yourself. You do not have to have the same attorney for your health and welfare and financial affairs. You may believe that one person is better placed to make welfare decisions for you and another would be more appropriate to handle the financial side.

It is not a cheerful subject, but once it has been put in place you can forget about it knowing that it is done. I would recommend that you have a lawyer help you with this process.

CHAPTER 3

Understanding your outgoings and creating a spending plan

Four of the financial mistakes discussed in Chapter 1 were failing to understand what your true outgoings are and prepare an accurate budget for the Form E, having unrealistic expectations of your lifestyle after divorce, failing to consider the impact of tax, inflation and investment returns and failing to develop a post-divorce financial plan. These are all attributable either directly or indirectly to getting the budget wrong.

If you are not used to dealing with the family outgoings, this will be a huge financial adjustment for you. It will also be extremely daunting. This chapter will walk you through the importance of having a spending plan and it will show you how to do it. This means that you will be able to produce an accurate picture for the Form E and you will also be able to cope once you are on your own with the finances. It's not until you are really on your own and independently responsible for your own financial security that you get a real appreciation of the importance of an accurate and realistic spending plan. This forms the basis of financial planning.

Why do I need to be clear on what I spend?

The first reason is so that you can work out exactly what you spend for both you and the children for the Form E, which will be the basis of the settlement agreement. The figures that you produce for the Form E will need to include absolutely everything that you spend, both essential and non-essential. Section 4 of the Form E asks you about the standard of living that you enjoyed during the marriage and getting the answer to this correct is absolutely key to ensuring that your settlement reflects this.

Most of us have no real idea of exactly what we spend and it is always a lot more than we think. Many of us know exactly what we earn but have no idea where all of our money goes. This is because we are not keeping track of what we spend in the form of a budget. When you have limited financial resources, you suddenly become very aware of what you are spending.

Failure to pay utility bills over time can result in you having services, such as gas, electricity and telephone, cut off. Failure to pay credit card bills and mortgage payments will result in issues with getting further credit in the future and if mortgage payments are missed it can eventually result in you losing the roof over your head.

Getting really clear on your spending from the get go will set you up in the right way for your new life and save you a lot of stress and worry further down the road.

How do I get clear on my outgoings?

Spending diary

The first step to getting clear on the outgoings is to understand exactly how much you are spending. The best way to get a handle on this is to keep a spending diary. You will need to be really disciplined to do this and you will feel massive resistance to doing it, believe me. For a whole month you need to write down absolutely EVERYTHING you spend. From coffees to lunches to hairdressers, you need to record it all. You will be shocked by how much you spend on things without even thinking about it, everyone always is! Don't freak out about it or punish yourself, praise yourself for being disciplined and writing it all down. There are also many different iPhone applications that enable you to record your spending on the go; I use one called Money Lover, which is pretty simple. There are many to choose from though.

Bank statements

Your spending diary will give you part of the picture and will encompass groceries, petrol, children's clubs and treats and other non-essential items. The rest of your outgoings are the household bills, which will probably have gone out of a joint account by direct debit and you will not have paid a lot of attention to. You now need to get to grips with these, so get the last three months' bank statements and a set of coloured marker pens. You need to mark up in one colour all payments to mortgages, credit cards, loans and other debts. In another colour you need to mark up gas, electricity, phone, broadband, water, sewage, sky, TV licence and council tax. The next colour will be for savings, pensions and life assurances, house insurance, car insurance and any other insurance. With the next colour you need to distinguish groceries, petrol, cleaner and other household spending. Then it's the children's outgoings, childcare, school fees, clubs and clothes. Finally, mark everything else with a different colour.

Creating a spending plan

The next task is to take the bank statements and spending diary and put the figures into the following tables. You will need to make them all into monthly amounts, so if you pay for something weekly, you need to multiply it by 52 and then divide by 12; if it's fortnightly, multiply by 26 and divide by 12; if it's 4 weekly you need to multiply by 13 and divide by 12. If it's quarterly you need to divide it by 3. You get the picture.

One expense that people always massively underestimate is the cost of food and household shopping. Always overstate the grocery spending as it certainly won't be decreasing with the way that food prices are rising.

Debts	£
Mortgage	
Credit cards	
Unsecured loan	
Secured loan	
Hire purchase	
Car loan	
Other debts	
Total	

Utilities	£
Council tax	
Electricity	
Gas	
Water	
Sewage	
TV License	
Home phone	
Broadband	
Sky/Virgin	
Mobile	
Miscellaneous	
Total	

Savings/insurances	£
Pension	
Savings account	
Childrens' savings	
Regular investment	
Buildings & contents	
Life insurance	
Medical cover	
Critical illness cover	
Income protection	
Pet insurance	
Travel insurance	
Car insurance	
Misc insurance	
Total	

Groceries/ petrol/ household	£
Food	
Other household	
Cleaner	
Petrol	
Travelcards	
Miscellaneous	
Total	

Children	£
Childcare	
Nursery fees	
School fees	
University fees	
Living costs (uni)	
After school clubs	
Other clubs	

Lifestyle	£
Hairdresser	
Beautican	
Other beauty	
Lunches	
Dinners	
Shoes	
Clothes	

continued…

Children	£	Lifestyle	£
Clothes		Handbags	
Miscellaneous		Other shopping	
		Holidays	
Total		Entertainment	
		Gym	
		Theatre	
		Cinema	
		Spa days	
		Massages	
		Horses	
		Days out	
		Total	

The bad news is that the lifestyle table is the 'non-essential' spending table. These are the things that you may have to cut back on once you are separated; you may also not be able to spend money as freely on the children either. This is where you are likely to notice the differences in your lifestyle and, indeed, you must accept these differences. However, for the purposes of the form E, make sure that you record absolutely everything that you spend. The court will aim to put both parties back in the position they were in before divorcing; therefore, the form E needs to capture everything.

These figures will form the basis of what goes in the Form E and your financial adviser will be able to insert these into their cash flow software to produce some assumptions about the effects of inflation. I will explain inflation in greater detail in both the savings and the investing chapter.

Once you have done this, acknowledge yourself for this achievement. It was a lot of work and will really help you in the future. Were you shocked at how much you spend?

Sources of income before and after the divorce

The next area to have a firm grip of is your sources of income and the regularity of this income.

For the Form E, you will need to add any income that you currently receive of your own.

- Are you working? You will need your last three payslips and also your most recent P60, which most people receive at the end of April or the beginning of May each year.
- Are you running your own business? You will need your accounts and you will also need to know what you have earned so far this year.
- Do you have any income from family trust funds? You need to add this onto the Form too. You will either need to ask the trustees to provide this to you or you will need to check the last year's worth of bank statements.
- Do you have any investments in your own right that you are receiving income from? You need to add this income too.
- Do you have rental properties? You need to add the rental income or your share of it if you own the property jointly with your husband or someone else.
- Are you receiving any pension income? Private and state pension income will need to be taken account of.
- Don't forget child benefit and any other state benefits that you receive.

Put all of the figures in the following table making sure that you use the right columns for the frequency that you receive money.

Income Sources	Weekly	4 Weekly	Monthy
Salary			
Bonus			
Self-employed			
Directors Salary			
Directors dividends			
Child benefit			
Other state benefit			
State pension			
Private pension			
Trust income			
Rental income			
Investment income			
Savings accounts			
Money owed			
Miscellaneous			
Totals			
Annualised figures			
Grand annual total			

Once you have added the figures into the columns you will need to annualise the figures. Weekly multiply by 52, 4 weekly multiply by 13, monthly multiply by 12, bi-monthly multiply by 6, quarterly multiply by 4 and 6 monthly multiply by 2.

Bi-monthly	Quarterly	6 Monthly	Annually

Once the annual figures have been calculated, your financial adviser can then calculate the net income after tax and national insurance (if you pay it).

This is truly an excellent step forward and will make such a great difference to you and how in control you feel. It is a great achievement.

From this, you will be able to clearly see what your income shortfall is and will be clear on exactly how much you need from your ex-husband. It will then be possible with a financial planner to calculate the amount of maintenance or lump sum you need to produce that income, taking into account tax, inflation and investment returns.

Once the divorce process has been finalised and you have received either a lump sum settlement or are receiving maintenance, you will be able to calculate exactly what income you have to spend each month. You can then prepare a proper spending plan.

There is a financial rule of thumb for a spending plan known as the 50/20/30 rule.

- No more than 50% of your money should be spent on needs. These are your essential living costs such as gas, electricity, water and sewage, groceries, home insurance, and debt repayments.

- At least 20% of your money should be spent on savings, pensions and over payments on debt.

- No more than 30% of your money should be spent on wants and this includes everything else in your outgoings.

Another way of looking at it is that 20% of your monthly income should be put away into savings, pensions and over payment of debt and the remaining 80% covers the rest of your outgoings. This will afford you financial security rather than financial worry. There is nothing more stressful than being in a position where you are living beyond your means or spending every penny that you receive without putting anything away for the future or a rainy day.

Get into the habit of putting away 10% of everything that you receive immediately that you get it. Put it in a separate account and don't touch it for any reason. It's amazing the difference this makes to your feeling of financial well-being. A great book to read around the mindset of money and for more information on the power of getting into the habit of putting money away is John F Demartini's How to Make a Hell of a Profit and still go to Heaven.

Now you are clear on your income and outgoings, the best way to manage your money, in my opinion, is to have more than one bank account. I have two bank accounts, one for my bills and one for groceries, petrol and the rest of my spending, but you may even feel the need for three.

My suggestion for splitting your bank accounts is to have the following;

Account 1 – Debts, utilities and savings / insurances, fixed regular children's costs

Account 2 – Groceries / petrol / household

Account 3 – Lifestyle

By separating your outgoings like this you will ensure that you don't accidentally spend bill money on lifestyle things, which is really easy to do if you think that all of your bills have gone out only to find that you had forgotten something.

Have your income come into your lifestyle account, and then set up a standing order to transfer the money that you need into the other two accounts as soon as the income has come in; then you know that what you have left in your lifestyle account is yours to spend.

Being vigilant can save you a fortune!

Many of us waste thousands by overpaying for our utilities and insurances. A bit of time and research can save you an absolute fortune. Here are some tips to save you money.

Do not stay loyal to the same utility company for your gas and electricity. Go on to www.payingtoomuch.com or www.moneysupermarket.com and compare providers. You will need to know how much gas or electricity you have used in the past year to enable a comparison, but for a bit of effort, you can save hundreds of pounds. Look out for the cost of the standing charge, which you must pay every month, regardless of how much energy you use, as a high standing charge can really catch you out.

On the subject of utilities, don't waste energy by leaving lights on and leaving things on standby. Also, leaving the heating on when you are not in the house is a huge waste of money. Some vigilance here can shave a load of money off your bills.

Have your water put on a meter rather than just paying the average. If you are a household that tends to shower rather than bath, and if you think about water consumption, you can save yourself a fortune by having your water put on a meter.

Shop around for telephone and broadband packages and don't just stay with BT. You can save yourself a fortune by shopping around for the best phone and broadband package. You can compare broadband providers at www.uswitch.com.

Don't pay for mobile phone insurance. It's an absolute waste of money, you can claim for a phone on your contents insurance if it is lost or stolen.

On the subject of mobile phones, make sure you shop around between providers for the cheapest deals on line rental and calls, as there is a significant difference between them. If you are buying a contract for a new iPhone you are better off paying a lump sum towards it and getting a cheaper a contract as it will save you money in the long run.

If you call Sky and threaten to leave them they will usually miraculously chop a massive amount off your bill, sometimes as much as half; likewise with Virgin media. It's amazing what they can suddenly come up with when they think they are going to lose you! In fact, do you actually need Sky at all? A freeview box has many of the popular channels and it's free!

Check a comparison website for your car insurance and don't forget to look on the sites that don't come up in the comparison websites such as Aviva, LV, Admiral and Direct Line. You can save hundreds by shopping around.

Likewise with home insurance, don't just pay the renewal that you get through from your last insurer.

Shop around for travel insurance when you go on holiday and don't just accept the quote from the holiday provider.

Make sure you use discount vouchers. If you are making a big purchase, do your research for the cheapest price and then check to see if you can get a discount voucher for it.

Don't keep a balance on a credit card when you have savings to pay it off. You will be getting hardly any interest on your savings but will be paying a fortune in interest on debt. Chapter 4 covers debt in detail and chapter 9 gives more detail about savings accounts.

Sign up to receive the newsletter from www.moneysavingsexpert.com as Martin Lewis is a genius at finding ways to save money. I have saved myself a fortune by following his advice.

The importance of an emergency fund

My final word on the spending plan is that it is absolutely essential to have an easily accessible emergency fund. This is not a slush fund to dip into for clothes and shoes! This is a fund that you can access if you have an emergency, such as the boiler breaking, the car breaking down or you having to find money for something for the children.

This fund should be equal to at least three times, but preferably six times your monthly outgoings and be in an instant access savings account. I will cover different savings accounts in chapter 9. You must NOT dip into it for other spending though; therefore, it needs to be sufficiently out of mind so you are not tempted to spend it, but also easy to access in an emergency.

CHAPTER 4

Debt – Let's get really clear

In the last 20 years debt has become a huge problem in our country and it is thanks to us all living way beyond our means that we are in such a deep financial crisis. Dealing with money is something that I wish I had been taught at school and, in particular, the dangers and reality of having too much debt. So I want to use this chapter to educate you on what debt is, what it costs and what to do if you have got yourself in a pickle with it all.

You may not have any debt and know that you will never have any, and if this is the case, please skip this chapter. If, however, you are likely to have a credit card or other debt in the future then this will teach you all the things that we were never taught as young girls.

As discussed in chapter 2, you need to firstly break all joint debt ties with your husband; anything that he does will have a significant effect on you. You are both liable for the whole debt in a joint account, and so if he defaults, the creditor will come after you. Do not accept him saying that he will pay a debt off as part of the settlement because you are still liable for it. Make sure that unsecured debts are repaid before the divorce is finalised. I appreciate that this may not always be possible but you must be mindful of the potential consequences.

Once you have had a joint debt with someone, even a bank account, you will have a financial association with them on your credit file. If they then get a bad credit rating by missing payments or defaulting, it can affect your ability to get credit. Once you have separated and paid off or split all of your joint debts, you can apply for a financial disassociation, which stops you from being financially linked going forward and his credit behaviour affecting yours.

What is debt?

Debt is any borrowing of money from a person, bank or any lending institution. However, it also includes bank accounts, mobile phone contracts, catalogues and 'buy now, pay later' deals.

They agree to lend you a certain amount of money in return for you repaying that money with interest within a certain period of time.

The interest rate is usually described as the annual percentage rate, or APR, and this includes any costs associated with that borrowing over the term of the loan.

You will usually need to pay back this money via a monthly payment and this can be either a fixed payment or can vary.

Variable payments can be affected by changes in interest rates or the cost to the lender of borrowing the money from the money markets. Banks and other lenders borrow money from each other on the open market and the rate that they can borrow it at will depend on how high a risk their borrowers are deemed to be.

What is the process for borrowing money?

If you decide that you need to borrow some money, you will be asked to fill out a credit application. On this application the lender will want to know information about your personal and financial situation so that they can assess whether you are a good or bad credit risk and whether or not to lend money to you. They will be assessing several areas and these are;

Affordability

In assessing this, the lender will need to know what income you have from all sources. You will need to tell them about maintenance income, rental income, employment income and any savings and investment income that you receive.

They will also need to know about your financial commitments so they will ask you about mortgage payments, as well as the amount outstanding and monthly payments to any other borrowing that you have. They will also need to know about any other financial commitments you have, such as utility bills and childcare.

This allows them to assess whether you can afford to take on the debt that you are applying for.

Credit worthiness

Every time you borrow money, whether on a credit card, a mobile phone contract, a catalogue or mortgage or loan, your repayment history is stored on your credit file. Remember back to chapter two where I told you that one of the first things that you should do is get a copy of your credit file to check whether your husband has taken out credit in your name that you didn't know about? Well, this is the record that lenders will check when they are assessing whether to give you credit.

The lender will contact the credit reference agencies electronically and check your credit file for certain information. The credit agencies will give you a credit score based on certain criteria, and the higher your score, the easier you will find it to obtain credit.

They will be checking against certain criteria, namely;

- Address history; your credit file will contain a record of all of the addresses that you have lived at where you have been registered on the electoral roll or obtained credit. They can also use this to verify that you are living at the address given in the application. If you have changed address frequently, this will have a negative impact on your credit score.

- Amount of debt you currently have; if you already have a lot of credit, whether that be a lot of different credit cards or loans, credit cards, mobile phones or catalogues, this will be seen in a negative way and impact your credit score, particularly if your credit cards are permanently near to their credit limit. If you have a load of different borrowings and everything is maxed out, the chances of you getting any more are pretty slim.

- Missed payments; if you miss a payment on a credit card, loan, mortgage, mobile phone bill, catalogue, buy now, pay later deal or any other borrowing it will show on your credit file. The odd missed payment on one account isn't the end of the world, but if you have more than one month, or missed payments on several items of borrowing, it will have a negative impact on you getting further borrowing in the future.

- Defaults; if you have missed several payments, usually more than three months consecutively, the lender will pass your account to a collection agency. This is known as a default and will seriously affect you getting any sort of credit in the future. A default stays on your credit file for six years, and during this time, you will struggle to get any form of credit as you are seen as too high a risk to lend to. No lender wants a borrower who may not repay what they owe.

- Consecutive applications for credit; every time you apply for credit it is noted on your credit file. If you make several applications for credit in quick succession, this can have a negative impact on your credit worthiness in the lenders' eyes.

- Employment; if you have recently changed jobs, it can have an impact on you getting credit, and certainly if you have changed jobs frequently as they will have concerns over the stability of your income and your ability to repay.

- Going from being employed to self-employed or starting a business is likely to have a big impact on your credit rating as you have no stability of income in the eyes of the lender. You will usually need to have been in business for two or three years and have accounts to show the lender before you can obtain credit. This is particularly true for getting a mortgage.

What are the common ways to borrow money?

Bank Overdraft

This is the simplest and most common way of borrowing money and, in fact, most people forget that an overdraft is actually borrowing!

When you open a current account with your bank, you will usually be given the option of having an overdraft. This can be anything from £100 to thousands of pounds, depending on how much money the bank sees going through your account on a monthly basis, and, of course, that all important credit score.

An overdraft facility is always there and you are able to dip in and out of it as and when you need to. The interest rate that is charged for using this facility varies between the banks and your credit worthiness and can typically range from 9.9% and 19.9%, which is a big variation so do your homework.

You can also apply for a fixed term overdraft for a big purchase, which will need to be paid back within a certain period of time. Personally, I think there are cheaper ways of borrowing money than this, and if you need money for a fixed period of time, you are probably better to get a personal loan than use an overdraft as it is likely to be cheaper.

The biggest piece of advice with your overdraft is to see it as an emergency facility and not part of your monthly spending. Don't fall into the trap of being constantly in your overdraft as it is difficult to get out of this habit.

Credit Cards

A credit card is a line of credit that allows you to make purchases now and pay for them later. You are provided with a card that you can use in shops, over the telephone or online and you are billed for the purchases each month. You will have a credit limit, which can vary between hundreds and tens of thousands of pounds depending on the criteria discussed previously.

The benefit of using a credit card is that you can have up to 56 days' interest free credit, depending on the lender, between you buying the item and paying it off in full. You also have protection on your purchases over £100, via a fab bit of law known as Section 75 of the Consumer Credit Act 1974, which means that the credit card issuer has to take equal responsibility with the supplier for the purchases you have made. So, if you do not receive something you have bought, it is faulty or the supplier goes bust, the credit card company has to reimburse you. It is, therefore, wise to make significant purchases, such as holidays, furniture and electrical items, on your credit card. Even if you only pay the deposit on the credit card, as long as it is over £100, the card company have to reimburse you for the full price of the item!

The secret to using a credit card wisely is to have a direct debit set up to pay off the whole amount every month, which means that you won't have to pay any interest and your purchases are protected.

If you think you can trust yourself to pay off your credit card every month and use it wisely then it is worth looking around for a credit card that offers you incentives, such as cash back, air miles or other rewards, as these can be valuable over time. They are, however, completely pointless if you are paying a whopping great load of interest.

If you do not pay off your credit card balance in full every month you will have to pay interest. Credit card interest tends to be around the 13% to 20% APR mark, which is, I am sure you will agree, a whacking great amount of interest to pay. If you have a credit card that is designed for those with less favourable credit scores, then you could be paying as much as 30% APR, which is just bonkers.

The other trap that is easy to fall into is the 0% credit card. You get a card that has 0% on purchases for the first six or nine months so it feels like free money as you don't have to pay any interest, and then suddenly you get to the end of the 0% period with a large balance and get hit with a load of interest.

Paying the minimum payment each month is the absolute worst thing that you can do, as you are paying off such a tiny bit of the balance that you are mainly just servicing the interest.

If you do get to the point where you have a balance on your credit card that you can't pay off immediately and you are at the end of a 0% rate deal, the best thing to do is a balance transfer. This is where you transfer the balance of one credit card to another credit card with a 0% deal. You then close the card that the balance came from and make sure that you pay off the balance on the new card by the time the 0% rate ends. If you keep doing balance transfers and not paying off the balance or worst still, you end up spending on the card that you transferred from, you will end up with too much credit and too many applications and you won't be able to do it anymore, meaning that you are stuck with a balance on a card and paying a lot of interest, which is when credit cards become dangerous.

You must always bear in mind that every time you use a credit card you are borrowing money and will have to pay it back; it is not free money or an extension of your bank account.

My advice to you is to have just one credit card that offers you something useful like air miles, cash back or vouchers for something that you will actually buy. Set up a direct debit to pay off the full balance every month and use it for holidays and other large purchases. Don't fall into the trap of using it for anything that you can't afford to pay for immediately and don't ever use a credit card to pay for your mortgage or other debt payments.

If you think you are going to need to borrow money on a credit card and not be able to repay it straight away, make sure you have done your homework and get a card with the best rates. Get a 0% deal and make sure you pay it off during the term of the deal. If you make just the minimum payment to a credit card with a £3,000 balance, it will take you 27 years to pay it off!!

Store Cards

Store cards are a form of credit card but for use usually within a specific store. So, for example, House of Fraser, Harrods, John Lewis and all the major department stores have them as well as the big national clothing and furniture stores.

Most of them only allow you to shop within their store with the card and they may provide some special offer, such as a discount on goods with the first shop or vouchers.

Store cards have absolutely massive APRs, usually upwards of 25%, and are ridiculously expensive if you don't pay them off. They don't have any other use, other than falling within the Section 75 rule that other credit cards fall into, which will protect your purchases.

If you were to make a very large purchase and the discount offer was large then I would probably take the offer and buy the item, pay the balance and close the card again immediately.

Don't get caught in the trap of having a load of store cards as well as credit cards because you are likely to get in a right old pickle trying to manage it all.

Buy Now, Pay Later deals also known as Hire Purchase or HP

You will commonly come across this on furniture and electrical goods where you go into the shop and see a sign saying that you can take it away today and pay for it at a later date. You may be offered interest free credit for a specified period of time, say a year or two. After this time you will usually end up paying a huge APR, which is again upwards of 25%.

The deal will usually be that you pay a small deposit and then make a monthly payment for a set period of time until you have paid for the item. If you pay it off during the term of the 0% period then the credit hasn't cost you anything, but if you go past that, you will be charged a huge amount of interest.

These types of offers, I believe, are to encourage people to buy goods that they can't afford and are out of their price range.

It's just another debt though and another addition of noise on your credit file. Offers like these are part of the reason why the country is in such a bad way debt wise and I believe should be avoided at all costs. If you can't afford it, don't buy it!

'Pay day' loans

Over the last few years, loads of companies have been popping up offering short term or 'pay day' loans to people who are short of cash. Some that come to mind are Wonga.com, payday

UK and quickquid.co.uk. They allow you to borrow usually between £100 and £1500 on a short-term basis, which is usually a matter of days and up to a month.

I have one piece of advice as far as these are concerned, DON'T EVER EVEN THINK ABOUT GETTING ONE OF THESE!

The APR on these loans ranges from 1734% to 4214% and more; yes, you read that right! 1000% APR!

Unsecured Personal Loan

This is a borrowing from the bank that is not secured on your house. You can borrow up to £25,000 over a term of up to seven years. Typically, these loans are for something such as the purchase of a car or other big purchases, such as improvements to your home.

The bank will assess your credit risk and the amount that you are borrowing and the APR is usually set accordingly, but is typically between 7% and 12%, although a lot of banks have lower headline rates in the current climate.

The benefit of borrowing money via a personal loan instead of a credit card, apart from the fact that it is a lot cheaper, is that you know exactly how much you will be paying and how long you will be paying for. This means that you can budget accordingly and you won't get any nasty shocks of hikes in interest rates or changes in their terms and conditions, which the credit card companies can do at will.

If you repay your loan early you are likely to suffer an early repayment penalty as the banks have calculated how much money they will make from you when they offer the personal loan, and by you repaying it early, they lose out on some of that interest. Repayment penalties vary between the banks and if you borrow money and think you will repay it early, you should ask them what the penalty is.

Also, beware of the deals that say that you don't have to pay anything for the first three months as you will still be charged interest over those three months and it just ends up costing you more.

The interest rates charged will vary from bank to bank and you should do your research on www.moneysupermarket.com and find the best deal rather than just going to your bank. Banks used to look after their customers and give them good deals, but that doesn't seem to be the case anymore, so it doesn't pay to be loyal. Be a 'rate tart' and find the cheapest deal.

Mortgage

These will be discussed in detail in chapter 7 so I will cover only briefly here.

A mortgage is a loan that is secured against your property and the lender takes what is known as a first charge against your home. This means that in the event of death or bankruptcy, the mortgage lender has the first right to the proceeds from the sale, which means that they are most likely to get their money back.

A mortgage is usually the cheapest form of borrowing as it is a long term loan and there is security for the bank attached to that lending in the form of your house, which is why the warning is always that you could lose your home if you do not keep up with repayments.

Secured Loan

The final form of lending that I will cover in this chapter is the secured loan. This is sometimes called a second mortgage and is a loan that is secondary to a mortgage and is secured on your property. This should be an absolute last resort and not a decision to be taken lightly.

The danger of this borrowing is that, because it is secured on your property, if you had problems repaying, you could and would lose your house.

You can borrow very large amounts of money depending on the value that you have in your home, known as the equity. This is the part of your house that doesn't have any borrowing secured against it. You can typically borrow between £10,000 and £100,000 over a term of between 3 years and 25 years.

Also, because you can borrow over such a long period of time, the temptation is to extend the borrowing in order to reduce the monthly payments. This is false economy as the longer you take to pay back the loan, the more interest you will pay and more it will cost in the long run.

You can either get a secured loan from your bank or mortgage provider or from one of many companies that have popped up over the years offering them. Daytime TV seems to have adverts constantly offering you secured loans and payday loans.

The companies that specialise in offering secured loans charge a fortune and it ends up costing you as much, and usually more, than an unsecured loan, which is much higher risk for you and lower risk to the lender. The amazing and worrying fact is that there is currently very little regulation of secured lending as it falls outside the scope of the consumer credit act and is not covered by the rules governing mortgage lending, so these companies seem to get away with charging what they like.

The average cost of these secured loans seems to be between 11% and 15%, which is very expensive, and for people with a poor credit rating the cost is over 20%! You can get cheaper borrowing on a credit card that isn't secured on your house! The lender will take what is known as a second charge on your home and this means that they are second in the pecking order to get paid on death or bankruptcy after the mortgage lender. I do believe that a secured loan should be a last resort, and if you can borrow money on an unsecured basis, that should be your first port of call. If you need to borrow more than you can get via an unsecured loan, then speak to your mortgage lender about increasing the size of your mortgage.

The negative effects of compound interest

The effect of compound interest is very powerful and it is important to understand how it can impact you. The best way to explain it is by using the following example:

You have a borrowing of £10,000 at an interest rate of 10%, let's assume for the purposes of this that you have had the debt for three years and you have not been able to make repayments.

At the end of the first year, you will owe £11,000.

Over the next year, you will accrue interest at a rate of 10% on £11,000, so by the end of the year, you will owe £12,100.

Over the next year, you will accrue interest at 10% on a balance of £12,100, meaning that by the end of the third year you owe £13,210.

As you can see, compound interest is very powerful and increases debt very quickly. It is, therefore, so important that you do not allow interest on debt to roll over and that you ensure you pay off interest and capital on debt.

We are not taught these things as young women and, so, unless we are financially trained, do not understand the dangers.

What if I can't afford to pay?

Unfortunately, this can happen to the best of us. Changes in circumstances can leave us in a very precarious financial position.

The first thing that you must do is face it and not bury your head in the sand. Burying your head in the sand is human nature and we all do it when we don't want to face the reality of a bad situation. But the only way to get to the bottom of and past a problem is to face it head on and push through it.

If you do not get a handle on debts as soon as possible, they can spiral out of control very quickly and you can find yourself in a terrible position, particularly where compound interest is concerned.

It's ok to feel scared and even panic. It is normal, just allow yourself to feel it and then commit to facing it and doing something about it. There are several options open to you.

Firstly, you need to decide whether or not you are in debt crisis. Are you in a position to pay your debts and manage minimum payments, or are you in a position that you are unable to afford repayments?

Debt refinancing

If you are in a position that you have a lot of debt but it is not at crisis point and your credit file is still in a good position, you can probably refinance some debts onto a cheaper deal.

Have a look at the debts you have and the interest rates that you are paying on each. Then get online and do a bit of research to see what rates other lenders are offering.

If you are paying interest on a credit card, get it switched to a 0% deal so that you are paying off the balance rather than just interest.

Look at refinancing personal loans so that you are paying the cheapest rate possible. Also, when was the last time that you checked what rate you were paying on your mortgage? You may be able to save yourself a load of money by remortgaging to a better deal. You need to check whether you would have repayment penalties if you are in a fixed rate deal though.

Speak to the lenders yourself

Having experienced this myself when going through cancer treatment, I found that some try and be helpful but most of them are distinctly unhelpful. I now think of banks as the guy that will offer you his brolly when the sun is shining and ask for it back when it starts to rain!

If you have a mortgage and have not taken a payment holiday before, this is your first port of call. Most lenders will allow you to take a holiday for three to six months and this can give you the breathing space you need to get yourself back on your feet. However, you need to remember that they will still charge you interest even when you are not making the payments and this will be added to the loan, and interest is charged on that interest so, again, it is not a decision to be taken lightly.

It is worth giving your credit card and loan providers a call to see if they can help you by freezing interest or putting payments on hold. However, as I said, I found the experience of the different lenders to be very mixed and this was quite a stressful process.

These next solutions are for a debt crisis situation and are serious solutions, which will have a long-term impact on your credit rating and your ability to get any sort of credit in the future.

Debt Counsellors

These guys will give you advice about budgeting and will also help you to write to the lenders to ask them to freeze interest payments or make an agreement for you to pay back certain amounts each month. Some of them are free and work on a not-for-profit basis and some of them are running it as a business to make money.

- Christians against poverty is one organisation and, although it's a Christian charity, you do not have to be religious to get help from them.

- There is also www.moneyadviceservice.org.uk, which is a free service and will be able to help.

- www.stepchange.org used to be the Consumer Credit Counselling Service (CCCS) and are also a charity organisation who will not charge you for help and advice.

Debt counsellors will talk you through several options which include budgeting and getting yourself on track, writing to your creditors to get them to agree to freeze interest and charges, an individual voluntary agreement known as an IVA or full bankruptcy.

Once you enter into the realms of any of the final three agreements you will be seen as a bad credit risk and it will affect your credit rating for years to come.

The step of writing to creditors to ask them to freeze interest and charges is a step in between an IVA. It is still a very serious measure though and should not be taken lightly.

Individual Voluntary Agreement (IVA)

This is the next step before we get to full bankruptcy and is very serious. Many people seem to undertake this thinking that it will get them off the hook with their monthly payments without realising how serious it is and what affect it will have on getting credit for years to come. An IVA means that you are insolvent and cannot meet your liabilities. You will not be able to obtain any credit while you are under the terms of an IVA. This will stay on your credit file for six years after the date that the IVA started.

So what is it? The debt counsellor will look at your current financial situation in terms of your income and outgoings and what liabilities you have. They will then write to all of your creditors and make an arrangement with them that you pay back a certain amount each month to each creditor. They may agree with the creditor that you pay back a reduced amount. A term will be set, over which you will need to pay back the creditors, and a monthly amount will be set. This could be over a term of, say, five years.

When you reach the end of an IVA, you will receive an IVA completion certificate, which is signed off by an insolvency practitioner, and is your proof that you have paid everything off and have a clean bill of health.

The next thing that you will need to do is obtain your credit file from the three credit reference agencies and ensure that there has been no other adverse credit history noted on your file and if it has, get this addressed immediately. You do not want to have anything else hanging over that six year mark. Once the six years is up, from the beginning of your IVA, you can obtain credit again, although it's very unlikely that you would want to after going through that ordeal, but it's worthwhile knowing that you can if you need to.

Bankruptcy

This is the final stage of debt problems and really is the last resort when all else has failed.

Once you have filed for bankruptcy you will lose EVERYTHING except basic possessions. You will lose your home, your car and any other valuable possessions. If you have a business, this will be shut down and your staff will be dismissed. It is incredibly serious.

It will cost you around £700 to go bankrupt to pay court charges and solicitors fees.

Once you have been made bankrupt, the court will deal with your creditors and any pressure will be taken away from you.

However, you will have to start again and will not be able to obtain any sort of credit, or even rent a property as the landlord will require a credit check, so you will have to apply for council housing.

If, though, it has got that bad that you can't cope and you can't pay your bills then it is an option that will take a lot of pressure off you. People have been known to say that the relief they felt after being declared bankrupt was huge.

You also need to bear in mind that certain types of employment will not be possible if you have been made bankrupt.

Again, a bankruptcy will stay on your credit file for 6 years, after which time you will be clear to start again.

I really think that it is so important to be educated around the dangers of debt; it is something that we were not taught as youngsters and I firmly believe that it should be taught. During the last boom period we all had debt thrown at us by the banks, credit card and loan companies and have been encouraged to live way beyond our means in order to consume more. This is the reason why we are in such a deep recession that will take years to come out of. By understanding the reality and dangers of debt, I hope that I can help you avoid being in this position. Before you buy something, always ask yourself: Do I really need it? Can I afford it? If the answer is no, don't buy it however beautiful it may be. Spending money makes you feel better for about five minutes, find a better way to make you feel good.

CHAPTER 5

Pensions are important, get your share

The biggest financial mistake you can make in a divorce is to not take your share of the pension or to take the house in lieu of the pension. You must consider your future financial security when looking at the assets on a divorce and not just take a short-term view. A pension fund can grow over the years and provide you with an income in retirement and, even better, it's a passive income that doesn't have extra costs attached to it. A house that you live in will not provide you a retirement income; in fact, it will only cost you money in repairs, maintenance and mortgage payments. I cannot express enough the importance of taking your share of the pension. Of course, every case is different and I am assuming here that you are able to make a claim against your husband's pension.

In this chapter I am going to explain the basics of a pension, what it is, why you need one and a brief description of the different ways that you can take an income at retirement. I will try and keep it as plain English as possible and not frazzle your brain! I will then go on to describe the different types of pension that your husband may have and the different ways that a pension can be split in a divorce. Pensions are, by nature, complex and so I fully understand that your eyes will glaze over as you read this information, but I want you to have some understanding of what you are likely to come across so that when it is discussed as part of the divorce it will not be completely alien to you.

What is a pension?

So let's start with the absolute basic question of what exactly a pension is. A pension is a tax efficient way of saving for your retirement. You are allowed to pay a certain amount of money into this pension each year, and as a reward for saving into it, the government will give you some tax relief. You can put either the equivalent of your gross annual earnings or £50,000 (2014/2015) per year into it, whichever if the lesser. So, for example, if you earn £30,000 a year, you could, in theory, make a contribution of £30,000 into your pension. If you earn £100,000 a year, you could make a maximum contribution of £50,000. If you do not work, you are allowed to pay in £3,600 per year.

If you are employed, you should be offered a pension scheme via your employer. In fact, it has now become law that everyone who is employed must be enrolled into a pension scheme, and depending on the size of the company that you work for, this will come into force between 2012 and 2018.

The money that you save into your pension is then invested for you in any number of ways depending on how comfortable you are with certain investments. The investments can grow in a tax advantageous environment until you get to retirement.

Why do I need one?

The basic state pension is currently £110.15 a week and that is if you qualify for a full state pension. Would you want to try and survive on that in retirement? I know that I wouldn't. If you take the house in lieu of your husband's pension, and you do not have a pension or any other savings or investments of your own, that is what you will be living on. I often hear people say that their house is their pension, but I am not aware of supermarkets taking bricks in payment for food! The house that you live in cannot provide you with an income unless you downsize and, even then, you would need to take a huge amount of equity from it to provide a fund large enough for a decent income. Taking the house in lieu of the pension because you have an emotional attachment to it is simply madness, which is why I discussed at the beginning of the book about taking the emotion out of the financial decision-making. A pension does not have to be the only method of providing a retirement income if you have other investments and a rental property portfolio, but it should be a starting point and certainly not walked away from in a divorce settlement.

What is the benefit of having a pension?

When you make a payment into a pension you get what is known as tax relief. What that means in English is that the government rewards you for saving for your retirement by not making you pay tax on that part of your income.

So, using the previous example: you are working and earning £30,000 and have decided that you would like to pay £10,000 into a pension. You actually only need to make a contribution of £8,000 because the government will pay in £2,000, which is a refund of the tax that you have paid on your earnings.

If you earn enough to make you a higher rate tax payer and you are not making the contributions straight from your salary, you will need to fill out a tax return as you will get some more tax relief this way, known as higher rate tax relief. If you make the contributions straight from your salary via your employer, you will get the tax relief immediately and don't need to do anything else.

The other important point to note is that you are only able to get tax relief on money that you have actually earned through employment or self-employment. Rental income, maintenance income and investment income are not valid for pension contributions.

The investments within the pension fund are sheltered from tax, which includes income tax (except 10% dividend tax), capital gains and, subject to certain rules, usually inheritance tax. This makes them a very useful vehicle for tax planning as long as you don't need to access the capital before retirement.

When can I get my money out?

In return for the tax breaks that you get for saving into a pension, the government expect you to save this money for your retirement. You are allowed to access your pension fund from the age of 55. However, the longer you can leave that fund to grow, the better. Most people expect to retire in their mid to late 60s. You actually don't ever have to take an income from your pension if you don't need to, but for the vast majority of us, it will form an important part of our retirement savings and so we will need to take an income from it once we retire.

What do I get when I decide to retire?

Once you get to the point that you are ready to retire fully and draw your pension you will have some options available to you. You will be able to draw 25% of your pension fund as a tax-free lump sum, which you can then use as you like. You may use this money to pay off the remainder of your mortgage or you might invest it elsewhere to give you another source of income, you might give some money to the children or spend it on holidays.

The remainder of your pension fund must be used to buy you an income and there are two main ways of doing this from a personal pension.

Fixed or secure income

Until fairly recently the only way to take an income from a pension was by buying what is known as a lifetime annuity. It is still the most common way of taking an income but it does have both its advantages and drawbacks.

A lifetime annuity guarantees to pay you an income for the rest of your life in return for you giving the provider a sum of money. Annuities are offered by the big insurers and a couple of specialist retirement companies. They are known as a secure fixed income because they guarantee to pay you an income for the rest of your life. There are a few bells and whistles that can be added to them, such as inflation linking and spouses' benefits and guarantees, but they are pretty straightforward. The advantage of them is obviously the security element and, once you have purchased your annuity, you know exactly what you are getting every year and you don't need to think about it again. If you smoke, drink heavily or have health issues, you will get a higher income as the provider assumes that you won't live as long as someone who is healthy and doesn't smoke or drink. The great advantage is that if you live until you are 110, you will not run out of income! The disadvantage of an annuity is that if you die early into your retirement, other than some income guarantees, that whole fund is lost and it can't be passed to your family. The other problem is that if interest rates are very low, like they are currently, when you retire, you will lock yourself into a poor income for the rest of your life. Once an annuity is taken out, it can't be changed and your family don't get a refund if you die young. Your money goes into a pool and the people who die young fund the people who live a long time.

The income that you receive from your annuity is taxable in the same way as your earned income was.

Unsecured income or drawdown

This method of taking income from a pension was introduced around 10 years ago and is fast becoming a popular method for those with larger pension funds who are happy to accept risk.

This method gives far more flexibility than an annuity in return for accepting risk to your pension fund.

Rather than purchasing an annuity, the fund stays invested and you are able to draw chunks of your pension out as an income, hence the term drawdown (drawing down). You can either take a prescribed level of income, which is driven by legal allowances, or for those who already have an annual pension income of at least £20,000, it is possible to draw out the whole fund subject to tax. The idea being that, because the money is still invested, the fund has the potential to grow. The income that you are taking is reviewed every three years, and if either interest rates and /

or your fund value has grown, you will get a higher income. Of course the reverse is also true, if interest rates and fund values have fallen, or the government tinker with the amount you are allowed to withdraw, you could find yourself with a much-reduced income. This has happened to people currently using this method. The other risk is that if you do live longer, you run the risk of running out of pension fund to buy you an income. However, if you die early into your retirement, your fund can be passed to your beneficiaries, subject to a hefty tax charge, but at least they get something. There is much flexibility and many options available for taking your income this way, but it is not an option for the cautious or the risk averse. The income that you receive is taxed in the same way as your earned income was.

Why is it so important for me to share my husband's pension on divorce?

The pension is often one of the biggest financial assets in the divorce, especially if your husband has valuable employer pensions.

If you have given up work to have children or stopped working when you got married, you will not have been building up a pension fund in your own right. You may not have had a pension fund of your own before you were married, particularly if you were working for a smaller company or you didn't opt in to a large employers' pension scheme. If this is the case, what are you going to live on when you retire?

In Chapter 1, common mistakes numbers 15, 16, 17 and 23 all relate to failing to understand that you must take your fair share of your husband's pension and failing to consider your long-term security. It is so important to take a strategic and long term view when looking at the assets of the marriage and ensure that you have enough to live on – both now and in the long-term. If you have been at home bringing up the children and have not had the ability to make your own meaningful pension savings, you have every right to share your husband's. The other consideration is your earning capacity in relation to your husband's. Are you realistically ever going to be able to earn the sort of money that he can? If not, then you are probably entitled to take more than 50% of his fund.

This is your future financial security and something that is not replaceable if you do not get it right when agreeing the settlement. I cannot impress on you enough the importance of taking this seriously.

Your husband will not be happy about it and especially if he has a final salary pension as he knows the impact of giving some of it up. You will be encouraged to offset other assets in lieu of the pension. DO NOT do it! It is very difficult to quantify the true future value of a pension to ensure a fair offset. If you take the marital home instead of the pension, you have just ended up with an asset that is going to cost you money in repairs and maintenance and won't provide you with an income in retirement meaning you have given up your future income, which is just madness.

The tricky part is calculating how much of the pension you should take and when a final salary pension is involved, therefore, getting an accurate reflection of the future value of it. The current value of it is not as important as the future value and the income that can be taken in retirement; this is why it can be so difficult to get it right. You will need input from both a financial planner and an actuary if the pension is a final salary scheme, and if it is a money purchase scheme, a financial planner using cash flow modelling software will be able to do the work.

What are the different types of pension that I may come across when getting divorced?

Pensions fall essentially into three categories – personal pensions, occupational pension schemes and overseas pensions. Due to the various governments constant tinkering with them over the years, there are many different contracts each with their own rules and nuances. The government attempted to simplify them back in 2006 and, I think, only succeeded in making them even more complicated! They have since tinkered with them constantly and made them continuously more complicated and difficult to understand. I am not going to attempt to explain all of the different types of occupational schemes because I will need a whole book to do that! I am going to give you an overview of the different personal pensions as that is what you will end up with in the settlement and so it makes sense to have an understanding of those. I will also explain the difference between a defined benefit and defined contribution occupational or workplace pension scheme, as it's important to know the difference. As for the many variations of defined contribution occupational scheme, I will name them so that if you come across them you will recognise the name, but I am not going to write a definitive guide because I know that you will have lost the will to live after reading even this much! Overseas pension schemes are incredibly complex, so I will give you an awareness of them but no more than that.

Personal Pensions

Personal pensions fall into three main categories, which are a SIPP, a personal pension and a stakeholder pension. I will explain each one in turn.

Self-Invested Personal Pension (SIPP)

If your husband is investment savvy, he may well have a SIPP. This type of pension wrapper gives the investor the greatest flexibility. You can invest in practically anything, except residential property within a SIPP. Investments that are commonly found within a SIPP are individual company shares, portfolios that are managed by a discretionary fund manager (more on this later) or commercial property.

The advantages of a SIPP are that they offer great flexibility in terms of what can be invested within them and larger fund values are often invested in a SIPP so that a professional fund manager can manage them on a bespoke basis. They are also the wrapper that provides the greatest flexibility when it comes to choosing how you can take your retirement income.

When it comes to divorce, property held within the SIPP can cause a big problem. This can cause a real problem if you decide to split the pension. Firstly, the property will need to be valued to provide a value for the Form E. If the market is depressed at the time, this is likely to severely undervalue the true value of that investment. It also does not take into account the future value of the rental income that will build up in the fund and significantly increase its value in the future.

The next problem will be how to deal with the property within the SIPP. The property does not necessarily have to be sold, there is another way around it, but this would mean that you co-own the property in a pension fund of your own and it would not provide a clean break. It would also cause problems if one of you wanted to sell the property in the future.

The other problem that could be encountered is the investments that are held within a bespoke portfolio managed by a fund manager as they could have included investments that are not liquid and easy to disinvest (cash in).

This is why it is absolutely essential to have independent financial advice by a trained pension specialist adviser.

Personal Pensions

The most commonly held pension that is not an employer pension is a personal pension. It is likely that your husband will have several of these dotted about if he has not had regular financial reviews with a financial adviser.

A personal pension is generally much simpler than a SIPP to split as it will be invested in various types of managed funds but cannot hold property or be managed as a bespoke portfolio by a fund manager.

The problems that can be encountered when splitting this type of pension are: firstly, if the fund contains a type of investment known as 'with profits', which tend to be found in older contracts. These types of contracts can often have certain guarantees, but also penalties for transferring out of them, so this will need to be taken into account when looking at how to split them.

If your husband has set up a pension more recently and the adviser was paid by commission, there will usually be significant penalties for taking money out in the early years. Some providers, particularly in older contracts, have penalties on transfer in any event.

Stakeholder Pensions

Stakeholder pensions were launched by the government in 2001 to encourage people with no or low incomes to save for retirement. The idea was to provide a contract with low charges and no penalties that was accessible to all. The investments that can be accessed within them are more restricted because of the low charging environment meaning that some fund managers, who have a lot of variety in the assets their funds invest in, could not manage their funds within such a tight cost structure.

Stakeholders can be set up for children and grandchildren, though, and you may come across these when you are looking at the assets.

The good news is that a stakeholder will be incredibly easy to split as there are no penalties on transfer and no complex investments that can be held within them.

Employer pensions

Employer pensions can be split into two main types, and these are defined benefit, which are also known as final salary schemes or defined contribution, known as money purchase schemes, which are the rest.

The defined benefit schemes are the ones that are likely to cause the greatest headache in a divorce, but are also incredibly valuable.

A brief overview of a defined benefit scheme

In its simplest terms, a defined benefit or final salary pension scheme will pay a guaranteed, defined income at retirement, which is affected by a number of factors; hence the name defined benefit. It will pay a percentage of either final salary, an average of the last few years salary or an average of the career earnings of your husband either at retirement or when he left the company. For every year that he is a member of the pension scheme he will secure a portion of his earnings as a guaranteed retirement income. This income is then adjusted so that it maintains its real value and isn't eroded by inflation. I will describe inflation in Chapter 10.

On leaving the company he will still have that guaranteed benefit. For example, I left employment with a company in 2008, but as I had built up nine years' worth of benefits in their pension scheme, I now have a guaranteed pension income from them, which I will receive at age 62, which increases each year to maintain its real value. This benefit is so valuable as I know exactly what income I will receive from them and I can tailor the rest of my retirement planning around this.

Defined benefit schemes are very expensive for an employer to run as they take the risk of ensuring that the pension fund can continue to pay its retirees for life. This is getting more expensive as people live longer. Therefore, many companies have closed their schemes to new members and some to existing members in an attempt to reduce their liabilities. So, if your husband has one, you absolutely need to ensure that you have your share of it because it is worth a fortune to you in terms of your future financial security.

The problem with defined benefit schemes is that the transfer value provided for the Form E is generally not remotely representative of the true future value of that pension, taking into account the fact that the income is guaranteed. I have seen some research done, which compares the value provided by the company with the value calculated by an actuary and they were wildly different.

This means that if you settle based on the figure provided by the pension provider, it could have a huge impact on your future financial security. It is absolutely imperative to have an actuary do the calculations; this is money that is absolutely worth spending. Your financial planner will then be able to add the actuarial figures into the cash flow modelling software to bring it all to life.

I won't blow your mind any further with defined contribution schemes other than to say that you absolutely should not walk away without taking your share.

Defined contribution or money purchase schemes:

A defined contribution or money purchase scheme is the broad term that mops up any other type of occupational or employer sponsored pension scheme. In simple terms it means that the amount of money being paid into the pension is defined and the income at retirement is not guaranteed as in a final salary scheme because the risk lies with the employee to build a big enough fund to provide their retirement income. The pension pots that your (ex) husband has may fall into the following categories: ABC Ltd Employee Retirement Scheme, an Executive Pension Plan (EPP), a Group Personal Pension (GPP), a Group Stakeholder Pension (GSHP), a Small Self-Administered Scheme (SSAS), a Group Self Invested Personal Pension (GSIPP), Additional Voluntary Contributions (AVC), Free Standing Additional Voluntary Contributions (FSAVC) or, coming into play over the next few years could be a pension scheme called NEST, which is an acronym for National Employment Savings Trust.

All of these schemes are basically a pot of money that, in most cases, can be split without too much hassle; the only two that could cause problems are the SSAS and the SIPP if they are holding land or property, or in the case of the SSAS, business assets.

However, as you can see, it's a bit of a minefield and all of the contracts will have slightly different rules and nuances and will you need advice to help you navigate. A financial planner using cash flow modelling software will be able to do this for you.

Overseas Pensions

If your husband is not British or is planning to leave the country, overseas pensions may come into the equation. This adds a whole other layer of complexity as you are dealing with non-UK laws. The problem being, that once you leave the UK and are dealing with another country's laws, they do not have to recognise a UK pension sharing order. It is not unknown for non-British husbands to transfer their pension rights to an overseas pension to avoid having to share their pension, and if this is likely to be the case, a court order will need to be obtained to prevent this happening.

There are five main overseas pensions that you may come across and they all have weird and wonderful acronyms. You may find a Qualifying Recognised Overseas Pension Scheme, otherwise known as a QROPS, or a Recognised Overseas Pension Scheme, called a ROPS, or a Qualifying Non-UK Pension Scheme, known as a QNUPS. You may also come across an Employer Funded Retirement Benefit Scheme, called an EFRBS, or an International Pension Plan, known as an IPP.

Confused? I am not surprised! Pensions are a complete minefield, which is why you need other professionals to help your lawyer!

State Pensions

The other important element to consider is your entitlement to state pensions. You have been bringing up the children, and while you are able to build up entitlement to a basic state pension, there are other elements to the state pension that you will not have been able to build up and you have an entitlement to share your husbands.

To give you a brief overview;

The Basic State Pension

As the name suggests, this is the basic pension entitlement and you will earn credits towards it, either through working or if you are claiming child allowance while bringing up children. There are other ways to build entitlement but these are the ways that are relevant to you. If you are not working and not bringing up children, you will not be building up any entitlement to this.

Assuming that a full allowance has been built up, at state pension age, which will be either 66 or 67 depending on your age, you will receive an income of £110.15 per week (2013/2014 rates). The government is looking at plans to introduce a flat rate pension of £140 a week, as there are different elements that currently affect entitlement for people who retire with no other pension benefits or savings to boost their incomes, which make calculation complex. This is not relevant to you, so for the purposes of this book I will not discuss it.

While this isn't a huge sum of money, it all adds up, and if you are entitled to it, then you should have it.

SERPS and The State Second Pension (S2P)

Depending on your husband's age, he will have some entitlement to The State Second Pension, or if he is older, SERPS also. SERPS stands for State Earnings Related Pension Scheme.

This can only be built up by people in employment so, as long as he is a director of his own company or an employee of a company, he will have rights building up.

This is an addition to the basic state pension and the amount paid out will depend on his salary over the years and how he has structured taking income from his company.

The important thing is that you will not have any entitlement of your own if you have not been working and you are entitled to your share of his.

In order to find out what your husband has built up, you will need to get a forecast from the Department of Work and Pensions (DWP) using a form called a BR19 (State Pension Forecast), which your husband will need to fill out and sign. They will then let you know what rights he has built up.

An important note to consider is that the state pension can only be split WHILE YOU ARE STILL MARRIED. This means that the split must take place before the Decree Absolute occurs or you will get nothing.

Methods of sharing the pension

So how can we go about helping you get your share of your husband's pension on divorce? There are three main ways of doing this and I will give you a brief overview of each way and some advantages and disadvantages of each.

Earmarking

This is an old method of pension sharing and is very rarely used now because of the significant disadvantages of doing it. However, as most pensions used to be on a final salary basis, it was a way of you getting your share of this.

Simply, the court would order that a proportion of the husband's pension rights would be earmarked for you. You would then be entitled to a proportion of the lump sum entitlement and a proportion of the income. This was fine when men stayed with one company for their entire careers, had to take retirement at a certain age and needed to draw the pension for themselves, but, nowadays, it is open to massive manipulation by the ex-husband.

The problem being that you have absolutely no control over this method of splitting the pension. You will not get your share until he decides to retire and he could decide to just not take the pension at all if he doesn't need it, meaning you have no income from it. The second way that it can be manipulated is that he could make a point of investing the funds in dreadful investments that lose money or make nothing, thereby destroying the value of the fund. Even if none of these manipulations take place, the income that you receive is taxed as if it was your husband's, meaning that if he is still an additional rate taxpayer in retirement, you will lose 45% of your income (2013/2014 rates).

This is, therefore, a method of pension splitting to be avoided!

Pension Offset

When using this method you agree to take more of the marital assets in return for your husband keeping his pension fund, so you are offsetting those assets in return for him keeping his pension rights. Mistake number 17 in chapter one is taking the house in lieu of the pension in a divorce settlement. This really is a huge mistake to make. As I have already mentioned, you cannot take bricks to the supermarket to pay for food in retirement. To give you a real idea of how much capital you need in retirement, a pension fund of £500,000, which would give you £125,000 tax free cash with the rest buying an income, would give a woman of 65 an annual income of approximately £21,500 before tax. This really isn't very much in comparison to the size of the fund. If you give up the pension fund, how are you going to raise that sort of capital? It is so important to take a long-term view.

Pension Sharing

This occurs when a court grants a pension sharing order, which gives you a percentage of your husband's pension pots as part of the divorce settlement. Your husband must then give you this proportion.

The usual outcome of a pension sharing order is that the agreed proportion of your husband's pension fund will be transferred out of his fund and you will need a pension contract of your own to transfer this into. This means that you now have complete control of this fund and can have it managed in any way that is suitable for you.

With certain company schemes, you may be able to become a member of their scheme but retire on your terms. It depends on the rules of the scheme.

This method offers a clean break with you having your own pension rights and this will give you some security for the future.

The disadvantages of this method of sharing the pensions are mainly in your husband's camp, in that he could lose income and fund guarantees. The other problem is that he could have assets within those portfolios that are not liquid and would be very difficult to split and share.

It needs to be considered that your husband could purposely transfer his pensions into non-liquid assets to prevent you from easily splitting his pensions, and if this is likely to be the case, a court order may need to be gained to freeze these assets to stop him from doing so.

There can be complications within the rules of the various pension funds and this is why you need a financial planner to help your lawyer with this process. I truly believe that this is the best method for you as you will have pension rights in your own name and not be relying on other assets for your retirement income.

CHAPTER 6

Don't get caught without protection

Financial protection is something that many of us don't have and yet we should all have it. I am a perfect example of why you should have financial protection and what a disaster it can be to not have it. As I mentioned in the introduction, I had to work throughout my cancer treatment because I had not protected myself financially. I only had myself to consider, I can't imagine how much worse it would have been if I had children too. I will explain the different types of cover available and why you need to protect not just yourself, but also the settlement with your husband if that includes maintenance or future lump sum payments.

What are the main types of financial protection that you need to consider?

Life Cover

This type of cover will pay out either a lump sum or an income on death, and there are three main types of cover to explain to you.

Term protection

This is life cover that is set up for a specified time period or term (hence the name). The term could be equal to the length of your mortgage, if the cover is to protect that, or it could be to cover until the children are a specific age, or cover until retirement age.

If death does not occur during this time, once the end of the term is reached, the policy will end and there will be no cash in value.

The policy will pay out a lump sum on death and is the cheapest form of life cover.

The main disadvantage of this type of policy is that if death occurred even one day after the end of the term of the policy, it would not pay a penny.

Family Income benefit

This is a type of term protection, which pays an income rather than a lump sum. It is set up for a specified term and is commonly used to cover the family income on death of a parent until the children reach a specified age; for example, on reaching 21 and finishing university. It may also cover until retirement. This cover could be used to protect maintenance payments in the event of early death of your ex-husband, if the agreement stated he pay maintenance for a specified period of time.

This cover is usually cheaper than term protection that pays a lump sum.

Again, the disadvantage of this type of policy is that if death occurred just one day after the policy ended, no money would be paid.

There is no cash in value with this type of policy either.

Example:

> Dianne and Paul have divorced and it has been agreed
> that Paul will pay Dianne maintenance of £3,000 per
> month, linked to inflation, until their youngest son John,
> who is currently four, reaches the age of 21 and finishes
> university.
>
> Dianne's financial adviser arranges a family income benefit
> policy, set up on Paul's life, which matches this agreement.
>
> Two years later Paul tragically dies of a heart attack.
>
> The family income benefit policy starts to pay out and
> provides Dianne with a replacement, inflation linked,
> monthly income until John finishes university at age 21.
>
> Had Dianne not had this policy, she would have no other
> way of replacing this income.

Whole of life policy

This type of policy is most commonly used for inheritance tax
planning and is a policy that lasts for the whole of your life, as
the name suggests. It means that there is no fixed term and the
cover will pay out on death, whenever that may be.

In the context of divorce, it may be used if your husband is
to pay you maintenance for the rest of your life or if there is a
disabled child to be provided for.

A whole of life policy is typically more expensive than a fixed term policy as the insurer will have to make a payment at some point, whenever that may be.

Policies can have an investment element to them with the intention of making the premiums cheaper by investing some of the money paid for the premiums in order to cover the higher costs of cover as you get older. These are sometimes known as unit linked policies. They may be what are known as pure protection, which means that the premiums you pay cover only the cost of providing the protection and there is no investment or risk element. My personal view is that pure protection with guaranteed premiums is the most sensible approach. It is more expensive at outset, but, in the long term, is actually cheaper as I don't trust policies that rely on investment returns not to have massive premium hikes in the future.

Critical illness cover

This type of cover will pay out a lump sum or an income on the diagnosis of a critical illness. So, for example, when I was diagnosed with breast cancer, as it was an invasive cancer and met the terms of the policy, I would have qualified for a full pay out of the sum that I had insured myself for.

Critical illness cover is most commonly paid as a lump sum and, as a minimum, should cover any debts. However, a critical illness can throw up all kinds of other issues and having extra money at this time can be a godsend. For me, I would have loved to be able to afford to go on holiday or to nice spas and treated myself while I was going through, and after, chemo. When I had finished treatment I was desperate to just go away on a nice long holiday to relax and unwind after so much stress, but I couldn't. I got a week away on a cheap and cheerful holiday and then got on with setting up my business. I would have also just liked to have a really nice sum of money as a buffer to give me peace of mind. Other critical illnesses could mean that adjustments need to be made to the house at large expense. You may have to go overseas for medical treatment and the money could be used to pay for this.

Critical illness cover can be set up either as a fixed term policy that provides a lump sum, which is the most common, as part of a family income benefit policy to provide an income or on a whole of life basis.

Critical illness cover is much more expensive than life cover as you are statistically more likely to need it. Many people, therefore, don't take it out because they feel that it is too costly and they can't afford it, but the truth is that you can't afford not to have it.

Example:

Mary had a critical illness policy for £500,000 of cover, which was to last until her 65th birthday.

At age 40 she was diagnosed with a rare form of cancer, which required her to travel to the US for treatment with the leading consultant.

Her critical illness policy paid out the full lump sum of £500,000. She was able to use this money to repay her mortgage and other debts, which totalled £300,000 and with the money left over, she could pay the £100,000 fees to travel to America for treatment. With the remaining £100,000 she was able to pay for adjustments to be made to her home to aid her after treatment as her mobility was much reduced.

Had she not have had this cover, she would not have been able to receive specialist treatment in the US and she would have had to continue to pay her mortgage and other debts.

Income Protection

An income protection policy will provide you with an income if you are unable to work due to illness or incapacity. This does not need to be a critical illness, just something which has meant that you are unable to work. This could be depression or an accident that has left you incapacitated. The cover will pay out until you either go back to work or the end of the policy term, which is usually retirement. The cover will start to pay out after an initial deferred or waiting period, which is most commonly three months, but can be immediate or up to two years. The length of the waiting period will depend on what sick pay arrangements you have through work and / or what resources you have to support yourself in the short term.

The amount of cover that you can have is typically 55% of your gross annual income, or if you do not work, there is housepersons' income protection, which will pay an income of £1,300 a month if you are unable to perform certain tasks (correct as at December 2012).

The policy used to be known as permanent health insurance because the policy does not end once you have made a claim. If you are subsequently ill in the future the policy will pay out again after the deferred period, until the policy ends.

Private Medical Cover

Private medical cover allows you to have medical treatment privately rather than on the NHS. Most big firms provide this as part of a flexible benefits package and so you will probably have been covered under your husband's policy.

You will be able to get treatment much more quickly with private healthcare, particularly for routine treatment and non-life threatening situations.

Having experienced both private and NHS treatment while going through cancer treatment, I can honestly say that the experience was far nicer in a private hospital. The NHS is amazing and the quality of the actual treatment is brilliant, it's the aftercare and the experience while actually in hospital that makes all the difference.

In a private hospital you have your own room and bathroom and have nice meals. The nurses are able to be more attentive and are less stressed. I had a lovely cooked breakfast after both of my first operations and had my chemo in a private room and was able to go home when I felt ready and able to. I could rest in peace while the chemo was administered and afterwards.

If you have treatment on the NHS, you are on a ward with other cancer patients, you have to share a bathroom, and when having chemo, you are in a room with other patients.

It's the surroundings you are in while you are having all this awful treatment that make all the difference, and for me, there is no comparison.

I had my mastectomy at an NHS hospital and it was, quite frankly, a horrible and stressful experience.

When you are going through something as stressful as cancer treatment, believe me you want the spa experience and not the rough experience!

Why do you need financial protection?

Many people think about having life cover to protect others in the event of their death and I fell into this trap too. I had protected my mortgage and debts in the event of my death so that my family could keep my house and not need to worry about paying off the mortgage, but I hadn't protected myself in case I lived! What an idiot!

If you have just been diagnosed with a critical illness, the last thing you need to be worrying about is paying the bills or paying for extra childcare. Knowing that you will receive a lump sum which will take care of all of those worries, and the peace of mind it will bring, cannot be underestimated.

As I mentioned in the section on critical illness cover, you can use the money to clear debts, pay for holidays, adjustments to the house, medical treatment or just have a nice lump sum sitting in your bank account to make everything feel a bit less stressful.

Income protection will ensure that your bills are paid while you are unable to work or if you are unable to look after the children as a stay at home mum. As mentioned before, this does not need to be a critical illness, it could be due to depression, an accident or some other illness or physical problem that is not a critical illness.

Again, the peace of mind of knowing that you have money coming in if you are sick or injured cannot be underestimated. These protection policies are worth their weight in gold, but many people do not appreciate their value until it is too late.

Housepersons' income protection is not a huge amount each month, but it will still make a difference if you are sick.

Life cover is important to ensure that your family are protected in the event of your death. Who would look after the children and would they have enough money to ensure that the children's standard of living would not fall? If the answer is no, you need to ensure that you provide for them in the event of your death. Life cover can also ensure that any debts are cleared so that you do not leave them to your beneficiaries.

As mentioned previously, the reason for having private medical cover is that you get to have the spa and not the rough experience when having medical treatment. It also means that you can be treated much more quickly and not have to wait months for a scan or a consultation. It really is priceless.

Why you need to insure your ex-husband

If your divorce settlement includes a maintenance payment from your ex-husband, which is common if he did not have enough capital to provide a lump sum for a clean break, it is important to protect this.

What will you do if he is unable to work and cannot make the maintenance payments or if he suffers a critical illness or dies?

Protection is absolutely essential and should be part of the settlement agreement.

By setting up income protection to protect this maintenance payment, you can ensure that, if he is unable to work, the maintenance continues to be paid to you until he either returns to work or his liability to you ends.

A family income benefit policy should be set up on his life to enable the maintenance income will continue to be paid to you in the event of his death until his liability would have ended.

If he is due to pay you maintenance for the rest of your life, you will need a whole of life policy to protect this.

Your solicitor can put forward a case that the settlement includes the cost of having private medical cover for you and your children, particularly if you had this in the marriage and it will be lost on divorce.

When setting up protection policies to cover the maintenance agreement, it is vital that you are the policy owner so that you know if payments cease to be made. Sadly, there are cases where this has not been done and the first the ex-wife knew that her ex-husband had not been paying the policy was when a claim needed to be made. You do not want to be in this situation so the right advice is crucial.

A word on trusts

I could write a whole chapter and, indeed, a whole book about trusts and their uses, but it would be far more information than you need! So, I am going to keep it really simple and tell you what you need to know.

A trust is in effect it's own legal entity, and because of this, it avoids all of the potential issues with wills and probate. This means that money can be paid immediately to beneficiaries meaning the right money ends up in the right hands at the right time.

Example:

Peter died on 5th March 2012, leaving a life policy of £500,000 in trust to Jane and their children. Due to the trust being in place, Jane was able to access the proceeds immediately and had the money in her bank account within a month.

Martin died on 1st December 2011, leaving a life policy of £300,000 to Helen, which had not been placed into trust. Helen could not receive the proceeds of the policy until probate had been granted, which took six months.

All life cover policies should be set up in a trust so that the money gets into the right hands at the right time.

Parties to a trust

There are three parties involved in setting up a trust:

The Settlor: This is the person who sets up the trust and places the assets into the trust. Once the settlor has placed the assets into a trust, they no longer legally own them.

The Trustees: These are the people that look after the assets in the trust and make the decisions about those assets. They are the legal owners of the assets of the trust.

The Beneficiaries: These are the people who are to benefit from the assets of the trust. There could be a single beneficiary or several beneficiaries.

There are three main types of trust which are used currently and they are a bare trust, also known as an absolute trust, a discretionary trust, also known as a flexible trust, and a life interest trust. There is a tonne of law surrounding trusts, but in simple terms;

A bare or absolute trust

Is set up for the absolute benefit of an individual or individuals, so it could be for just you, or you and your children. A split must be stated when the trust is set up and it cannot be changed. The beneficiaries cannot be changed once the trust is set up. It is basically set in stone, with no flexibility.

They are used because they are more tax advantageous than a discretionary trust and are fine when there is certainty over who will benefit and that it will not change. Once a beneficiary is over 18, they have absolute rights to the trust assets and can call on them at any time. Hence the name absolute trust.

A bare trust does not protect assets on divorce, so if your husband is the beneficiary of a bare trust, you have a potential claim on the assets as part of your divorce settlement.

A discretionary or flexible trust

This type of trust gives much more flexibility over who can benefit from the trust and no beneficiary or split have to be agreed at outset.

No beneficiary has a right to either income or capital from that trust. It is at the discretion of the trustees, hence the name discretionary.

These trusts can be very complex and carry significant tax consequences, although when used in conjunction with a life policy, can be relatively simple.

They are ideal if there is likely to be a change in beneficiary in the future and also to protect family assets from divorce.

Although the assets of a discretionary trust can never be given to someone who is not a beneficiary, they can be taken into account by the judge.

So, if, for example, your husband has been receiving a regular income and capital from a discretionary trust, the judge may consider that you should get a larger share of the marital assets to compensate for this.

A life interest trust

This is a type of trust where the beneficiary is entitled to receive an income from the trust for the life of that trust but has no right to the capital. Once that beneficiary dies or the terms of the trust have ended, the capital is left to a different beneficiary.

For example:

Margaret was married to Harry and it was a second marriage for both of them. Harry had children from his first marriage and wanted to ensure that on his death, he provided a home for Margaret during her lifetime, but that his assets were ultimately left to his children.

He therefore set up a life interest trust in his Will, which stated that Margaret had a life interest in his house and the income from his assets, but that on her remarriage or death, everything went to his children.

For the purposes of divorce, the income from a life interest trust can be taken account of in a settlement. It is, therefore, important that you are aware of any trust income that your husband receives.

CHAPTER 7

Understanding the assets

In chapter 1, some of the issues identified are a result of not understanding what different assets are, their risks and their ability to be turned into cash.

Depending on how savvy an investor your husband is, he may have a myriad of different types of assets and I want to educate you about some of them so that you can have a better understanding if you come across them.

The last thing you want to end up with is assets that you can do nothing with and have no real value to you. Likewise, you should not accept depreciating assets, such as a car, in your divorce settlement, no matter how much you like the car!

I have split the chapter into what I call liquid and illiquid assets. Liquid assets are those which can be easily made into cash, and illiquid assets are those which are more difficult, if not impossible!

Liquid Assets

Cash

The first and most simple asset is good old cash. You know exactly what it's value is, you can withdraw it from your bank account to pay for things and it is always readily available unless it is in a fixed term savings account (more on that later). When it comes to taking your share of the marital assets, cash is king.

Gilts

These are loans to the government. When they need to raise money to pay for things, or they need to increase cash flow into the economy, they issue gilts. A good example of this has been over the past few years with the economic downturn. The government has issued debt to effectively try and borrow its way out of the financial crisis.

An individual gilt pays regular interest, known as a coupon and the original investment back at the end of its term.

Gilts are viewed as being incredibly secure and are easy to buy and sell in the open market. For this reason they are very liquid assets.

Corporate Bonds

These are loans to companies. When a company needs to raise money for something it can issue corporate bonds. The security of these depends on the quality of the company issuing them.

As with a gilt, they pay regular interest (coupon) and the original investment back at the end of the term. These are, again, very easy to buy and sell in the open market unless they are for a company that does not look good financially. They are also very liquid when issued from good quality companies and are known as investment grade bonds. Bonds issued from companies with questionable finances, known as junk bonds, are unlikely to be very liquid.

Ordinary Shares

Most shares that are bought and sold on the stock market fall into this category. Buying a share in a company means that you own part of that company. Big companies may have millions of shares in circulation so the part of the company that you own is tiny. When the company has made profits it can pay dividends to its shareholders, although not all companies do this. You can easily sell these shares on the stock market. The value can go up and down quite significantly in a short period of time and so the value that you got them at can have risen or fallen significantly when you come to sell them. They are, however, very liquid and can quickly be sold for cash.

Stocks and shares ISAs (and ex PEPs)

A Stocks and Shares ISA is a tax wrapper that allows the investor to invest in stocks and shares without having to pay any tax on the gains that are made or the income received from any assets held within them (except 10% dividend tax). The amount that can be invested is subject to an annual limit and this changes each year.

A stocks and shares portfolio will be easy to cash in and so is a liquid asset. The investments held within it can be very volatile depending on what your husband has invested in, so this must be taken into consideration. If the amount that is transferred to you from your husband exceeds the annual limit you have available, you will lose the tax benefits of an ISA.

Personal pensions

Simple personal pensions will generally be invested in funds that are liquid and easy to split, with the exception of property funds or with profits funds. This has been discussed in more detail in the pension chapter, but was worthy of a mention here.

Discretionary Managed Investment Portfolios

These are portfolios that are managed by a discretionary fund manager who will have created a bespoke investment portfolio for your husband. This portfolio will have a variety of different types of assets within it, depending on how much risk your husband has taken. The assets can fall into both liquid and illiquid depending on what the fund manager has invested in. The fact that you are likely to have a different view of investment risk to your husband should be considered here. The fund manager may need some time to switch out of some of the investments within the portfolio to allow a split. This should also be considered.

Investment Bonds

These are essentially tax wrappers. Your husband may have UK based bonds, known as onshore bonds, or bonds that are based somewhere like Dublin or the Isle of Man, known as offshore bonds.

A straightforward bond that has been set up through as insurance company that contains their own funds will be liquid and fairly simple and easy to split, although there are some that can be problematic, such as with profits funds that can have penalties for early encashment. There may also be capital guarantees within these products that would be lost on early encashment, which is not a good idea if the stock market has fallen since the original investment was made. The problem with these sorts of bonds lies when the investments are managed on a discretionary basis and the fund manager has invested in something that is illiquid in the short term.

The other issue with splitting investment bonds is tax. There can be significant tax consequences on transferring a bond or part of a bond across to you and this will need to be carefully considered.

For that reason, bonds, I feel, straddle both camps of having the ability to be both liquid and illiquid.

Illiquid Assets

Here are the assets that I would consider to be illiquid and problematic in a divorce.

Property

Property can be highly illiquid if the market is depressed and it needs to be sold to provide cash in a divorce settlement. It can take months or years to sell a property and in a depressed market may have to be sold at a significant loss.

A straightforward transfer of ownership of an investment property will not be a problem liquidity wise, but can create a large capital gains tax liability as both sale and transfer of assets will trigger a potential capital gains tax liability. It depends whether you want to be left with an investment property to manage or want the simplicity of the cash. This can be a particular issue if the property is overseas. Do you want the hassle of dealing with a non-UK property? Property is an asset that will cost you money on an ongoing basis with maintenance and repair costs. This should be taken into consideration.

Land

This can be incredibly difficult to sell and be a real problem in a divorce settlement. If the land does not have planning permission for development or forms part of a farm it can cause a huge problem. You would need to have specialist knowledge of dealing in land and the area that you are dealing with to even consider this as part of a divorce settlement. Avoid at all costs and have it sold for cash before the divorce completes so that you know the true value of it.

Antiques, Art, Jewellery and Wine

These all fall into the collectibles category and can be incredibly difficult to value with any certainty as they are all so subjective. A specialist dealer from an auction house will need to value the items. However, once auctioned, the price achieved for them can vary dramatically depending on the market or demand for that item at the time.

In my view, anything that falls into these categories should be viewed as highly illiquid and difficult to get rid of. These are the sorts of items that you may be likely to have an emotional attachment to and this comes back to point 6 in the first chapter about bringing emotional attachments to assets and not thinking strategically. You have to take the emotion out of it and ask yourself the following questions:

How will having this item as part of a divorce settlement benefit my future financial security? What financial security am I giving up in order to keep this item? How will this affect my children and I? Am I realistically likely to sell it and release the cash value in the future?

Unlisted Shares and AIM shares

AIM stands for Alternative Investment Market and shares traded on this market are the shares of very small companies. Unlisted shares are shares of companies that are not listed on any sort of stock market and, therefore, there is no active market for them.

Either of these types of shares are extremely high risk assets and can be impossible to get rid of and release for cash. They should be avoided and not accepted as part of a divorce settlement. If your husband was prepared to accept the risk of buying them, then he should carry the risk of selling them and not you.

Tax Incentivised Investments

These are investments that are classified as high risk, but investment in them carries significant tax advantages designed to encourage investment into small businesses. They will generally fall into one of three categories and I will give a very brief explanation of each so you have a basic understanding.

1. Enterprise Investment Scheme known as an EIS

Your husband will have been able to invest up to £1 million into one of these and receive income tax relief of 30%. There are other significant tax benefits in holding an EIS, but in the interest of not overcomplicating things,

I won't go into detail here. The assets in an EIS are small companies that are high risk. There can be all sorts of weird and wonderful things held within them. The asset will need to be held for at least three years to benefit from the tax advantages. They should be viewed as highly illiquid and high risk as the companies within them can go bust. They are not designed to be sold in the short term.

2. Venture Capital Trusts known as a VCT

These are, in principle, very similar to the EIS in that the assets held within them are highly illiquid and high risk. Your husband will have received 30% income tax relief for investing in this as well as other tax benefits. He must hold the asset for at least five years to benefit from the tax breaks.

3. Seed Enterprise Investment Scheme known as SEIS

These are the latest tax incentivised scheme to be introduced by the government and are even higher risk than an EIS! The companies within in them must basically be tiny start-up companies. Your husband will have got 50% tax relief for an investment of up to £100,000 and will not be able to release his investment any time soon as it's a commitment to helping a small company start to grow.

SIPPs and SSASs

As mentioned previously in the pension chapter, these can be particularly troublesome to split in a divorce as they can hold land, property or shares in his business.

They could hold the property that your husband's business

trades from, or indeed, agricultural land, both of which can cause significant issues.

Business Assets

If your husband has his own business, this can be a real problem to split on divorce. Firstly, you will need to try and get a realistic valuation of the business, which can be difficult in a business that is fairly new and growing fast. It is also possible that your husband will try and hide business assets, which is where your private investigator will come in.

Once a valuation has been agreed, you will then need to be able to release your share, which in a business that is growing and does not hold much cash can be a real problem. You may need a forensic accountant to help with this. There are three main ways to value a business and these are looking at the earnings of a business, looking at the assets of a business or looking at the amount of dividends being paid. It is not unusual for a business to be valued at far less than you believed it to be, especially in the current financial climate. It can cost thousands to have a proper valuation done by a forensic accountant.

This is not an exhaustive list of the different assets that your husband may have but is designed to give you an overview of some of the more common assets that you may come across in a divorce. Depending on how sophisticated an investor your husband is and how much risk he is prepared to take, you may find all sorts of assets on his form E that you had no idea he had. Women tend to have a much more cautious approach to risk than men and so assets that he may find suitable for him are generally wholly unsuitable for you. As you can see, it's absolutely essential to have the relevant professionals involved in the process so that you can understand what he has and the true value and implications of each.

CHAPTER 8

Demystifying property

The traps to avoid on divorce

One of the biggest and most common financial mistakes that women make on divorce is hanging on to the marital home because they have an emotional attachment to it. This is detrimental in terms of both your emotional and financial wellbeing.

From a financial perspective, firstly, you may not be able to afford to run the house and pay the mortgage, which could have devastating consequences to you and your family. Giving up entitlement to other valuable assets, such as the pension in return for a house that is going to cost you money for repair, maintenance and mortgage servicing, is not a clever move.

Making a strategic financial decision of selling the marital home and moving into a smaller house that you are able to afford and accepting the change to your lifestyle will serve you far better in the long term and reduce your stress levels.

With regard to the emotional side, my clients have told me that they felt a huge relief once they moved out of the marital home, which they had not expected to feel. They were much better able to move on emotionally once they were in new surroundings.

In this chapter I will walk you through the things you need to consider when buying a property and the professionals that will be involved. Moving house is stressful and getting divorced is stressful, but having a clean break emotionally and financially will mean that you can start to move and get on with your new life.

What do I need to consider when buying a property?

What is your budget?

The first thing that you need to consider is what you can afford to spend on a property. Will you be buying the property outright or will you need to borrow money? How much money are you able to borrow? You need to get really clear on this before you even think about starting to look at properties. You need to remember that you will have other costs associated with the purchase, such as solicitors' fees, surveyors' fees, lenders' fees, stamp duty, removals and anything that needs doing to the house or furniture that needs to be bought. You need to factor all of these into your budget so that you don't end up overstretching yourself and putting in an offer on a house that you can't realistically afford. Once you have arrived at a realistic budget, you need to stick to it.

What type of property?

This needs to be carefully considered when thinking about the long-term repair and maintenance costs. The quaint, pretty little cottage or Victorian house is indeed beautiful but is likely to be a massive drain on your finances. They will cost more to heat and, because of their age, will have many things that are likely to go wrong and cost a fortune to put right. Things like dodgy electrics that need replacing, holes in the roof, damp, to name a few.

A new build may not be as pretty but it will be a lot more practical. It will have been constructed to be much more energy efficient, which will cost you less, and because it has been built more recently, there will be less to go wrong.

Again, it is important to take the emotion out and look at it strategically so that you don't get caught out with a massive repair bill that you can't afford in the future.

What are your needs, wants and deal breakers?

You need to be clear on exactly what you want and don't want from a property before you start looking. Some time doing this will save you loads of time and energy traipsing around houses that are not suitable. So, here is a table to help you make a list of what you absolutely need, i.e. minimum number of bedrooms, location to schools or stations, your wants, i.e size of garden, conservatory, en suite bathroom, more bedrooms, and your deal breakers, i.e. on a main road, in a rough part of town.

Needs	Wants	Deal breakers

Needs	Wants	Deal breakers

Location, location, location!

This is an important starting point both from a day-to-day living perspective and also the resale value of a property. The things that you need to consider are;

The quality of the neighbourhood; what is the crime rate like? You don't want to end up living somewhere that has a problem with burglaries or muggings, for example. What are your potential neighbours like? Are you going to end up living next door to the neighbours from hell? It is better to buy a smaller house in a better area than a large house in a bad area.

Travel connections; is the property near to a station? Is the station connected to a decent rail link? Are there good road links nearby? You don't want to end up being stranded in the backside of nowhere meaning you can't get to others and they can't get to you.

Schools; this is a huge consideration for the children. You need to research the catchment areas for certain schools, particularly in London. You don't want to end up being in the catchment area of a bad school. If the children are to have, or continue with, a private education this is less of an issue, as long as it's easy enough to get the children to and from school.

Conservation and greenbelt areas; these can be a real problem if you want to make any changes to your property later as you will find it near on impossible to get planning permission. Likewise with a listed property.

Chains, gazumping and other issues

Putting in an offer on a property is just the beginning of the process! Once the offer is accepted, it starts the process, which, unfortunately, has no guarantees of a happy ending.

In a buoyant market where there are a lot of buyers interested in a property, there is a risk of being gazumped. This is where someone comes along with a higher offer after your offer has been accepted, which is then accepted by the seller effectively dropping you out of the process. It is obviously highly irritating and unfair if you have already spent money on having the property surveyed.

The other issue that you may encounter, which can cause a sale to fall through, is being part of a large chain. This means that there are several people all buying and selling properties to and from each other and they will all have to complete at the same time on the same day. The more people there are in this chain, the more potential there is for problems.

If someone in a chain pulls out of a sale, it can cause the whole chain to collapse. It is best to try and find properties that are chain free as you will avoid this problem, and if not chain free, you need as small a chain as possible.

The parties involved in a property purchase

When buying a property there will be several parties involved, which is what can make it complicated and stressful. A large chain will only add to this. Here is a guide to parties that will be involved and some pointers to help you navigate.

The Buyer

That's you! Always remember this caveat – Buyer, beware! Ask questions and trust your gut instinct. If something doesn't feel right then step away. Unfortunately, there isn't much protection for buyers in the property market and you have issues as mentioned above with being gazumped and people pulling out of sales elsewhere in a chain and even a seller deciding to take a property back off the market.

The Vendor

That's the person selling the property to you. Again, trust your gut instincts in people. Personally, I would feel much more comfortable in buying a property from someone that had actually lived in it. Take someone else with you when you go to view a property, both from a security point of view and also because they won't be emotionally connected to a property as they won't be living in it and can be more objective. You could be buying a property that is brand new or hasn't been built yet. This is pretty risky in case the property never actually gets built and you have parted with money. Personally, I would avoid this unless you are buying from a very well-known firm or you have someone to help you who really knows the market.

The Solicitor

You will need a good conveyancing solicitor to take care of the legal side of buying a property and deal with any issues that arise. You cannot complete a property purchase without a solicitor, so you need to find one either before you start looking or as soon as you find a property that you like. In finding a suitable solicitor I would suggest that word of mouth is a good method of finding the right person. Your divorce solicitor or financial adviser should be able to recommend one to you if your friends don't know of anyone. If you are getting a mortgage, the lender will have a panel of solicitors that they recommend, and some insist on using these, so find out first.

The Surveyor

As part of a property purchase you will need to have a surveyor look at the property and write a report. This is mandatory if you are getting a mortgage. The surveyor will be looking at the structure of the property to ensure that it is sound and safe. They will point out any issues that they see or feel could arise in the future. This is so important as you need to know that the property you are buying is safe. If there are issues with the property you will need to negotiate with the buyer to get these rectified before the sale completes or give you a discount on the purchase price to do them yourself. You will need to get quotes for the cost of doing this work before you make any negotiations on price. It could be that significant issues arise from the survey, which mean that the property is not suitable.

You should always have a full structural survey done as it's vital that you understand any potential issues with your future home.

Your solicitor or mortgage lender will have a panel of surveyors that they work with and will be able to recommend one to you.

The Mortgage lender

If you are borrowing money to fund the purchase of a property, you will need to get a mortgage. I will cover this in much more detail in the mortgage section. However, some mortgage lenders will only deal with certain surveyors and certain solicitors and this can be helpful if you don't know anyone yourself, or can be a real problem if you want to use a solicitor of your own choosing. When choosing a mortgage lender, it is best to go through an independent broker who will be able to look at the whole of the market and get you the best deal rather than just going to your bank. You will need to have agreed borrowing in principle first so that you know what your budget is.

Stamp Duty

Stamp duty land tax (SDLT) is tax on the purchase of a property and is a big extra cost to consider when budgeting for buying a house. It is payable by the buyer on the day of completion of the property purchase. The amount of stamp duty you will pay depends on the cost of the property and the government are constantly tinkering with it, so by the time you read this book, it could well be different to the figures I have written here.

Purchase price or transfer value	SDLT rate
Up to £125,000	Zero
£125,000 – £250,000	1%
£250,000 – £500,000	3%
£500,000 – £1 million	4%
£1 million – £2 million	5%
Over £2 million	7%

★Source HMRC website – correct as at December 2012

The process of buying a property

This is a basic step-by-step process to navigating the purchase of a property.

Agree borrowing:

If you are getting a mortgage speak to a broker first and get an agreement in principle from a lender. This is an agreement to lend you money, subject to you finding a house that they are prepared to lend on. You will need the budget that you prepared in chapter 3, which will give you a clear idea of your income, outgoings and affordability. You will need to decide how much you can realistically afford to spend on a mortgage each month. It may be that the lender is prepared to lend you more than you feel that you can realistically afford and so you must stick to your budget. You may also find that you are able to borrow significantly less than you hoped for. This is the essential first step.

Set your budget:

You need to work exactly what everything is going to cost you so you don't get any nasty shocks. Doing the research upfront will save you a lot of stress later on the process. So work out what the stamp duty will be on the value of the house you are looking at. What are the solicitor's fees? What are the lenders' fees? What will the survey cost? How much do removal firms charge? Once you are clear on what all of these things cost, you know exactly how much you can spend on a property.

Research the area:

Once you know what your budget is, you can start to research the area(s) that you would like to live in. Looking at schools, transport links and neighbourhood.

You can look on websites such as www.aboutmyarea.co.uk to help you with this.

Arrange a solicitor

Find a solicitor that you feel comfortable with, or ask your lender who they use.

Start looking at houses

Now here is the fun / stressful bit! Looking at houses. You can find houses on websites such as www.rightmove.co.uk or www.zoopla.co.uk. This will give you the houses for sale in your area of choice. You can set a price range and choose some that you like the look of and then contact the selling agents. This will save you traipsing around estate agents.

My advice is to trust your gut feel when you look at a house. If you don't get a good feeling, move on until you find something that feels right when you walk through the door. Be patient, it can take a while to find something that you are happy with. It took me ages to find my house but I knew as soon as I drove up to it.

Putting in an offer

Find out how long the house has been on the market for. Always start with an offer below the asking price and work from there.

The longer the house has been on the market, the lower the offer you will get away with. In a buoyant market with a lot of buyers, you won't get away with too much. You need to consider any work that needs doing to the house or garden when putting in an offer as this will give you something to negotiate with, but you will also need to consider if you can afford to do the work and how it will affect your overall budget.

Instruct the Solicitor

Once your offer has been accepted, you will need to instruct your solicitor. It typically takes six to twelve weeks for a property purchase to complete. If there are issues it can take even longer.

Tell your lender

If you are using a solicitor recommended by your lender, they can instruct the solicitor for you.

They will also instruct the surveyor to look at the property.

At this point you will also need to speak to your financial adviser about protecting your mortgage with life and critical illness cover. Your financial adviser will ensure that everything is set up and the policy starts on the day that your mortgage starts.

The surveyor

Remember to request a full structural survey rather than the minimum requirement for the lender.

Deal with any issues

You will need to work with your lender / solicitor / vendor to sort out any legal or structural issues that arise as a result of the survey or legal searches. If there are issues that will cost money to rectify, you will need to re-negotiate the price with the vendor to take account of this. This is the part of the process that can really slow things down.

Exchanging contracts

This is the point where you will need to have your deposit ready. It is usually 10% of the purchase price. Once contracts have been exchanged and deposits paid you have a level of certainty about the sale completing, as if people in a chain pull out at this point, deposits will be lost. Once the exchange happens, a completion date will be set, which is typically a week later.

Completion day

This is the big sigh of relief day!

You will need to have transferred the rest of the cash to the solicitor the day before, which will include the stamp duty. The mortgage will be put in place and you can collect the keys from the estate agent. You will also need to get your life and critical illness cover started on this day.

A time will have been arranged with everyone as to when you can collect the keys and turn up with your removals lorry.

Welcome to your new home!

What do I need to know about mortgages?

Here is a guide to mortgages starting from the very basics.

What is a mortgage?

A mortgage is a long-term loan that is secured on a property. The loan is for a specified term, typically 25 years, but can be a much shorter period of time or longer in some cases. The term that you agree will depend on your age, the younger you are, the longer the term can be. Most mortgages will be set up to ensure that it is paid off by the time you retire.

You can get a mortgage from a bank, building society or specialist mortgage lender. It is best to get a mortgage through an independent broker as they will have access to the whole of the market and will know what criteria certain lenders have, which will save you a lot of time and hassle.

How do I get a mortgage?

When you apply for a mortgage, the lenders will look at certain criteria, such as the percentage of the value of the property you are borrowing, known as loan to value, your credit worthiness and your ability to make the repayments, known as affordability.

The effect of the financial crisis has made lenders much more cautious about lending money and they look at applications much more carefully.

The bigger your deposit, the happier the lender will be and the better the rates that will be available to you. The best rates tend to be for those with a deposit of at least 40% of the purchase price of the property because the lenders feel secure in the knowledge that if they had to repossess the property, there is a high likelihood of them getting their money back.

Creditworthiness goes back to the discussion at the beginning of the book about your credit file. Any missed payments, defaults or county court judgements will go against you. Defaults and CCJs will generally mean that you won't get borrowing as you are seen as too high risk. Likewise, if you have never had any credit, this can also go against you as the lenders have no track record to look at to see how good you are at making payments.

Affordability is also a huge consideration and the lender will need to take account of all of your income and maintenance payments to ascertain whether they think you will be able to afford to make the repayments over the term of the mortgage. Some lenders will not recognise maintenance payments as income and so won't take them into consideration when assessing affordability. This is why having an independent broker will save you a lot of time and trouble.

If the borrowing is for a rental property, the lender will look at whether the rent that you can get for that property will cover the mortgage payments.

How are interest rates set?

The interest rate that you are able to agree on your mortgage will be based on two main components;
The technical side, which looks at economic factors, such as gilt yields, long-term interest rates and what rates the banks are able to lend to each other.

The amount of risk you pose as a borrower will be the other main consideration. The higher the amount you borrow in comparison to the value of the property, the greater the risk you are perceived to be and the higher the interest rate the bank will charge you. The bigger the deposit you can put down, the better the interest rate will be.

What are the different categories of mortgages?

Residential

This is the mortgage that you will have if you are buying a property to live in yourself.

Buy to let

This type of mortgage is for a property that you buy as an investment to rent out.

Commercial

This is a mortgage on a commercial building, such as a shop or an office. If you are buying a property in a pension fund, this is the type of mortgage you will have.

Repayment or interest only?

A repayment mortgage means that you are paying back both capital and interest within your monthly repayments, and at the end of the term, you will have paid back the amount you borrowed. This means that you will have great peace of mind of knowing that at the end of the borrowing term the house will belong to you. You can make overpayments to your mortgage to pay it off faster meaning that you will reduce the amount of time that it takes to pay off your mortgage.

Interest only mortgages, as the name suggests, are paying only the interest element and not reducing the outstanding balance. This means that at the end of the mortgage term, you will still have the whole balance to pay off. This is not a situation that you would want to find yourself in.

Interest only mortgages were commonly taken alongside an endowment policy with the policy supposedly paying off the outstanding balance at the end of the term. Many low-cost endowments were sold, which relied heavily on investment returns that subsequently were not achieved, which triggered the endowment scandal that has been rumbling on for many years.

In the recent property and debt boom, many people took out interest only mortgages to enable them to borrow more money, and the lenders were not seeking proof of what the borrower had in place to enable repayment of the mortgage at the end of the term. This has led to many people having interest only mortgages with no clue about how they are going to repay them. Effectively, they are renting their house from the bank!

Banks have tightened this practice up hugely over the last few years and are now very cautious about allowing people to have interest only mortgages. A repayment mortgage will cost you more each month than an interest only mortgage because you are repaying capital as well as interest, but it means that you will not have an outstanding balance at the end of the term.

What are the different types of mortgage?

Fixed rate

A fixed rate mortgage will have an interest rate that is set at a certain level for a certain length of time and it will not change during that period. The fixed periods are typically two years and five years. So, for example, you may get an interest rate of 5%, which is fixed for two years. The benefit of a fixed rate is that you know exactly how much you will be paying for the term of that fixed rate, which will help you to budget. Also, if interest rates increase significantly during the term of the fixed rate, your payments won't increase as you have fixed them. The downside of a fixed rate mortgage is that if interest rates fall during the fixed term, you will continue to pay a higher amount. Also, if you have been enjoying a low fixed rate while interest rates have been rising, you may be in for a shock at the end of the term if your payment increases significantly.

If you repay a fixed mortgage early by either paying it off, overpaying or switching lenders, you are highly likely to have a repayment penalty, which can be significant. Therefore, a fixed rate mortgage is best if you know you won't be repaying early and if interest rates are low at the time you take the mortgage.

Variable rate

A variable rate mortgage has an interest rate that changes as the lenders' change their interest rates. You can either be on a lender's standard variable rate (known as the SVR), which typically happens when you reach the end of an agreed deal with them. So, for example, if you have been on a two year fixed rate, you will revert to their SVR at the end of the deal unless you change to something else. In the current climate, the lenders standard variable rates are reasonable in terms of cost because of the economic situation, but they are generally more expensive than an agreed deal.

Tracker mortgages

A tracker rate is a form of variable rate mortgage and the lender will set the rate to track an interest rate, usually the Bank of England base rate; so, for example, it may track at 3% above the base rate. That is fine when interest rates are low, but looks expensive as they start to rise.

It is best to get advice from a good broker as to which will be the most suitable mortgage for you, your circumstances as well as taking into account the current economic environment.

CHAPTER 9

All you need to know about savings accounts

Savings accounts are an important part of your portfolio of assets and are a must for your emergency fund. Here is a guide to savings accounts with all you need to know to help you choose the right one.

What is a savings account?

Banks need to borrow money from you to lend to borrowers, it's banking in its most basic form. They allow you to deposit money with them and, in return for this money, they pay you a rate of interest. You can either have your money back on demand or after an agreed fixed period. The interest may be paid to you monthly, annually or at the end of the term that you have put the money away for.

Why do you need one?

Leaving all of your money in a current account is daft because most of them pay absolutely no interest at all. So, by leaving it all in a current account, you are basically giving the bank your money for free, which they can then lend to others and make money on it.

You need to have your emergency fund money in a savings account that you can get to easily but not too easily. This should ideally be six months' worth of outgoings to be really safe, but three months' worth will suffice.

Planned spending money should also be kept in a savings account and this will include money for holidays, home improvements, a new car or a deposit for a house. The timescale of when you need the money and how quickly you will need to access it will drive the type of savings account you use and I will cover this next.

Cash is also an important part of an overall portfolio of investments as it provides liquidity, which we discussed previously. I will talk more about investing in the next chapter.

What are the different types of savings accounts that you will come across?

Variable rate

The most commonly used type of savings account is a variable rate savings account. Like a variable rate mortgage, the rate will change depending on the Bank of England base rate and other factors such as gilt yields.

The advantage of this type of account is that it is flexible, plus it's usually easy to access the money quickly. Rates can vary considerably depending on the type of account that you have and I will cover these in more detail.

It pays to be a 'rate tart' with savings accounts; don't just go to your bank because it's unlikely that they will give you the best deal. Go onto www.moneysupermarket.com and get the best deal. Banks do not reward you for loyalty these days.

Fixed rate

A fixed rate savings account will pay you a fixed rate of interest if you can put your money away for a fixed period of time, with the minimum usually being three months.

The interest is typically paid to you as a lump sum at the end of the term. The advantage of these sorts of accounts is that you will usually get a higher interest rate as banks have the certainty of having your money for a known period of time and so will reward you for this.

The disadvantage of these accounts is that if the interest rates go up while your money is fixed in one of these accounts, you can lose out considerably. You will not be able to access your money before the end of the term without incurring significant interest penalties.

There is no flexibility in these accounts so you need to be certain that you can put the money away without needing it for the term that you have chosen.

Traditional branch based savings accounts

These are the old style savings accounts where you have a passbook and go into the branch to pay money in and withdraw it. They went out with the dinosaurs!

They are extremely expensive for the banks to manage as they have to see you face to face and cover all the costs involved with that. Because of this, they pay you next to no interest. It's so low that you may as well leave it all in a current account. Apart from that, do you really want to be queuing up with all the little old dears collecting their pension every time you need to take some money out? No, I didn't think so; therefore, do not open one of these accounts!

Postal accounts

These are nearly as out dated as branch based accounts! Some banks do still offer them, but again, they are not the easiest way to transact. You will receive a higher interest rate than a branch based account because they are less expensive to run. These types of accounts usually have a waiting or notice period between you requesting a withdrawal and you getting the money. This could be anything between a week and 90 days.

Telephone based accounts

First Direct were the innovators of this type of account and now most telephone based accounts will also offer online access as well.

You will usually get a much better interest rate by using a telephone service as the costs are lower for the provider.

It is easy to access your money as the cash will be transferred straight to your current account. Depending on the provider you can make an instant transfer of up to £100,000.

Internet only accounts

These accounts will usually pay the very best rates of interest as the costs are so low for the provider. If you are comfortable doing your banking online, these are the best sorts of accounts in my opinion. You are able to transfer between the savings account and your current account online, and as long as you are sending less than £10,000, the transfer is instant. High amounts need additional security checks online and so will take longer.

ISAs (Individual Savings Account)

A cash ISA is a type of savings account where you do not pay any tax on the interest.

You can save up to half the annual ISA allowance in the cash element each year. For 2013/2014, the allowance is £11,520 and so you can invest £5,760.

You should aim to use your ISA allowances each year as you can shelter your savings from the taxman.

The interest rates paid on ISA vary hugely and it is best to review the rate regularly and keep checking www.moneysupermarket.com for the best rate. It is easy to transfer your ISA between providers so that you keep getting the best rate.

You can have either a fixed or variable rate ISA depending on whether you are able to put the money away for a set period of time without touching it.

Junior ISAs

You can put money away each year for each of your children that is sheltered from the taxman in a Junior ISA. You can invest £3,600 per year per child and build them a nice nest egg for the future or save for their university costs. You can either invest in cash, stocks and shares or a mixture of both.

National Savings and Investments

These are essentially government backed savings and have a 100% guarantee on your money.

The best known NS&I product is the premium bond. You can invest a maximum of £30,000 in premium bonds, and each month these bonds are entered into a draw to win a maximum of £1 million. There are a range of smaller prizes and the winnings on these are free of tax.

They also offer an ISA, a children's savings account and a variety of other savings accounts, although they have reduced their offer significantly in the current economic climate and you can get better rates elsewhere.

What are the risks of having money in a savings account?

There are two main risks to consider here and they are default risk and inflation risk.

Default risk

This means the risk of a bank going bust and not being able

to pay you back your money. Remember the queues outside Northern Rock when people thought they were going bust? Or the furore over the Icelandic banks going bust and people losing all of their money, including some local councils?

In the UK we have something called the Financial Services Compensation Scheme, or FSCS for short, and this gives you some guarantees. Each bank guarantees your money up to the value of £85,000. However, it is important to note that this only applies once to the parent bank in a group of banks. So, for example, if you had some money with Lloyds, Halifax and Bank of Scotland you would only get one lot of £85,000 as they are all part of the same group, Likewise with NatWest and Royal Bank of Scotland. So it's important to know which banks are part of the same group if you are spreading your money around for that purpose.

If you have a large amount of cash, it is advisable not to have it all in one place.

Inflation risk

In simple terms, inflation means an increase. In the context of this book and your finances it means the rising cost of living. So each year food, fuel, clothing, utilities and housing costs rise and sometimes these rises can be quite considerable.

If the interest rate that you get on your savings after tax is less than the rate of inflation then what you can buy with this money in the future becomes less and less. So, your money is losing its buying power all the time. It is rare for you to be able to get an interest rate after tax that beats inflation and certainly not consistently. Any inflation linked savings products that were around have been withdrawn because of the economic climate.

The longer you leave your money in a savings account, the more compounded the problem becomes.

So while savings accounts are great for your emergency fund and for planned spending, you should not use them to build your future nest egg as the value of your money will be destroyed by inflation.

Example:

To give you an idea of the effects of inflation over a ten year period, I have compared the effect on the value of £10,000.

> £10,000 in 1999 was worth only £7,246.38 in 2009. The effect of inflation over those 10 years being 32.69%
>
> Source: www.thisismoney.co.uk

The website compares the cost of a loaf of bread in those 10 years and the increase has been 147%! Other comparisons include cigarettes up 60%, petrol up 42%, house prices up 123% and the level of consumer debt up 158%. Scary reading! So while the average inflation has been around 3.2% per annum, certain items have increased by huge amounts meaning that if your money is not growing faster than inflation, it will have a devastating impact on what you can buy with it in the future.

CHAPTER 10

The (very) basic principles of investing

At some point during or after your divorce you are going to be in a position whereby you have to make some decisions about investing. We women are typically far more cautious than men about investing and come at it from a completely different viewpoint. Women who have not invested before generally feel very nervous about it and I am sure that you will be no different. So, in this chapter I am going to give you a basic understanding of investing so that by the time you sit down with your financial planner you will have some knowledge of what is being offered to you and can make an informed decision.

Getting advice

It's unlikely, but you may be asking yourself: why do I need advice? The answer is that money invested correctly, over the long term, can have a very positive impact on your financial security; however, money invested badly can mean substantial losses and even complete loss of money.

That's not to say that just because you received advice, you won't see your money go down, because, unfortunately, no one can guarantee that. But, good advice and the correct asset allocation for you is a great starting point. More on asset allocation later.

What can I expect from a financial planner?

Assessing your needs, goals and objectives

A good financial planner will have a long conversation with you about your plans and goals and what timescales you have in mind for achieving them. These goals may include sending the children to university, paying for school fees, big expenses for the children, like buying a house or getting married, as well as your own retirement objectives.

They will help you to calculate what the cost of that end goal will be and using the cash flow modelling software that I discussed earlier will help you build a picture of the true cost and effects of inflation and tax.

Once you have agreed your future goals and quantified them, you will need to look at what you have available now to help you achieve those goals. How much capital do you have? How much disposable income do you have? Are your income or outgoings likely to change significantly? Are you expecting any inheritance or other capital sums?

The lynchpin of financial planning, though, is the conversation around your outgoings and spending plan. Once you and your planner have a crystal clear knowledge of what you spend now and how that is likely to change in the future, a meaningful financial roadmap can be built. This will drive the conversations around investing, capacity for loss and will determine the required asset allocation.

Assessing your risk profile

The first job is to understand what previous investment experience you have had and whether it was a positive or negative one. The adviser will need to understand what types of investments you have previously had (if any) and what your knowledge and experience is.

Once they have gauged your understanding of different investments, they will need to fill in the gaps in your knowledge so that you are able to make informed choices.

The next step is to complete a risk-profiling questionnaire, which will give both you and the adviser an understanding of what is known as your attitude towards investing and risk. This will give the adviser information about your view of risk and your attitude towards the downside of risk. This is the starting point of the conversation around risk and investments and how you feel about investing.

Capacity for loss

The adviser will then need to assess and understand what is known as your capacity for loss, which looks at the effect on your financial security in the event of you suffering a short-term investment loss. This is an incredibly important part of the process and the adviser must take into consideration your reliance on the capital invested. If you are relying on your capital to fund your lifestyle and do not have a large asset pool, your capacity for loss will be minimal and you will, therefore, need to have your assets invested in very low volatility investments.

If you are investing for the long term and you do not need to live on your capital in the short term, or if you have a very large asset pool, you will able to tolerate short-term losses without the risk of it impacting your standard of living.

Apart from your physical ability to tolerate short-term investment losses, it is also important for the adviser to consider your emotional attitude towards investment losses; therefore, they must evaluate at what point you would feel uncomfortable in a market downturn. The most important part of an investment and risk conversation is to understand your attitude and feelings towards the downside of investing and then build the portfolio from there.

Creating your portfolio

Once your adviser is armed with all of the above information, they will be able to map a portfolio for you with the correct asset allocation. I will cover asset allocation in greater detail later in this chapter, but, essentially, it is the right mix of different types of assets, which are balanced to provide you with the best return for the level of risk that you are able and willing to take. The idea is to minimise risk and maximise the return. The adviser will also decide which tax wrappers are the most appropriate for you depending on your goals and current and future tax position.

Reviews

The key to good investing and financial planning is reviewing that portfolio regularly. As investments change and grow, the make-up of the portfolio will change. This is a natural occurrence because of the effects of the growth and decline of asset classes within your portfolio. It is, therefore, essential that your portfolio is reviewed and rebalanced regularly so that it continues to have the correct asset allocation for your risk profile.

The worst thing you can do is spend all that time and money at the outset and then never review it.

Your priorities will change as you go through life and events happen which will affect how you feel about how much risk you want to take with your investments and perhaps what your needs are from the money that you have; so, this will need to be discussed and taken into consideration with your adviser.

You should see your adviser at least annually, or more often if this is the service agreement that you have set with them. At these reviews you will look at your current financial position, any changes that have occurred since your last review, where you are in relation to your goals and any changes that need to be made to your financial plan to help you get there. Changes in legislation will also need to be taken account of as they may affect your financial planning.

Understanding risk and investments

Having an understanding of the elements of investing will help to make it less fearful, and so, in this part of the book, I have broken down the important areas of investments and risk that you need to understand.

What is risk?

The Wikipedia definition of risk is as follows:
Risk is the potential that a chosen action or activity (including the choice of inaction) will lead to a loss (an undesirable outcome). The notion implies that a choice having an influence on the outcome sometimes exists (or existed). Potential losses themselves may also be called "risks". Any human endeavor carries some risk, but some are much more risky than others.

Risk versus reward

The very basic concept of risk versus reward is that the more risk you are prepared to accept, the higher the potential reward you could expect to receive. So, if you were a real risk taker and happy to invest in a shoot the lights out kind of investment, you could expect to either make a huge loss or gain. If, however, you are a very cautious investor, you are never going to make a very big gain on your money, but you would hope not to see a large loss to your investment either.

Some risks you will come across when investing

Here are some of the risks to be aware of and terms that you will come across when investing your money. Some of these I have already mentioned in previous chapters, but to refresh your memory, I will explain them again.

Inflation risk

This is the risk that your investment and savings aren't growing at the same rate as the rise in the cost of living. So, if you were getting only 2% return on your money after tax but the cost of living was going up by 3% each year, your money would be losing its buying power; therefore, in real terms the value of your money is falling. To put it into context, £600 will buy you a great pair of Louboutin's in today's money; however, in 10 years' time, the same pair of shoes will cost considerably more because prices of the materials used to make them will have risen. So your investment needs to grow by more than the rate of inflation to make you any real money. This rise in the cost of living is measured by something known as the Retail Price Index, or RPI, and you will hear that mentioned on the news or in the paper.

Default risk

This is the risk that occurs when the company you are invested in is unable to meet its liabilities. So, remember the example of the banks not being able to pay the savers back their money?

That would be a default. In this case, the company is either in serious financial difficulty or has gone bust completely. If you cast your mind back to 2008, a big company known as Lehmans Brothers went bust due to the credit crunch. They guaranteed the investments of many other companies, and so when they went bust, the impact spread far and wide and caused lots of investments to default.

Another way to explain it is to imagine that you and your friends had all decided to have a bespoke outfit made by a small, upcoming designer and you had paid the money up front. The designer then got into difficulty or went bust altogether and was unable to pay your money back or give you the outfit. That is a default.

Thanks to this, investment managers are much more cautious about checking who guarantees what before investing, which is of great benefit to you who is only now starting to invest.

Liquidity risk

Liquidity in investing terms is the ability to sell an investment and turn it back into cash quickly. Some things can be sold quickly and others can take a lot of time. To give you an example, say you had some shares in Vodafone and you also had a property to sell. The shares in Vodafone could be sold in seconds and you could have the money in your account by the end of the day. The property, as we discussed, before can take anything upward of 6 to 12 weeks. So you can see that the Vodafone shares are much more liquid and easy to turn into cash than trying to sell a property.

So, in an investment portfolio, you would not want an illiquid type of asset if there were a chance that you may need to cash in quickly as you won't be able to.

Market risk

This is the risk of the whole market, i.e. stock market falling at the same or a whole sector falling. The easiest example of this to understand is what happened when the credit crunch hit in 2007 and 2008, and every investment plummeted with the fear and bad news that kept coming. I think of it in terms of greed and fear and a bit of a herd mentality. When things are good and people are making money, everyone wants to invest and the stock market gets pushed higher and higher. When things are going badly, everyone gets spooked and starts taking their money out, which makes the market fall and fall. The clever investor does the opposite to everyone else. So when the markets are really low and everyone is saying it's bad, think of it like the Harrods sale and take advantage of the cheap prices. However, when the market is high and everyone is investing, be cautious and think about moving to safer investments.

A whole sector can also fall due to a problem affecting all companies in that sector and an easy example is the banks. Because of the constant scandal and bad news that keeps coming from them, no one likes banks and so it affects all bank shares.

Sometimes a single company can be affected; for example, at the beginning of 2012, Burberry's shares were booming and the retailer was saying that they were having a great time in the recession. By September, they had issued a profit warning because their sales had fallen and so their shares dropped by about 20%. You wouldn't want to be selling the shares then as you could lose money, but they were cheap to buy.

The trick to investing successfully is spreading your money in the right way, known as diversification, and having investments that are affected by different variables so that you lower the risk. This is what you are paying your adviser to manage for you. I will explain this to you in greater detail later in the chapter.

What are asset classes?

The next area to understand is the different types of investment that make up a portfolio, known as asset classes. There are four main asset classes, which are cash, fixed interest, property and shares.

Cash

We have talked a lot about cash already and it is always part of a portfolio. The reason that all portfolios have an element of cash is because it provides liquidity. It gives the fund manager freedom to buy other assets quickly if they need to. Its downside, as mentioned before, is that it will lose its buying power over time because of the effects of inflation. Any money that will be required within a three year time period, whether that be for capital or income requirements, should be invested in cash.

Fixed Interest

This can mean either gilts or corporate bonds. I mentioned both of these in an earlier chapter, but to refresh your memory I will explain them again.

Gilts are a loan to the government and their correct name is gilt-edged securities. They are classed as a very safe investment as the risk of government defaulting is absolutely tiny, and if they did, we would all be in trouble as the country would be bankrupt! It is possible to buy gilts directly and hold them until they mature. The cost of a single gilt is £100, and this is also what is known as its face value. Most gilts have a maturity date at which the £100 is repaid and this can vary from a few years to more than 40 years. Some gilts do not have a maturity date and are known as undated gilts; these were mainly issued after the second world war. Each gilt will pay an annual interest rate until maturity, known as a coupon.

Corporate bonds are loans to companies and, again, have a face value of £100 and pay a coupon. The perceived risk depends on how financially stable the company is. You should only invest in what is known as investment grade bonds, which are loans to companies that are financially stable and considered to be a good investment risk.

Both corporate bonds and gilts are traded in the open market as part of a portfolio, and once they are traded, they behave differently. Their capital value will fluctuate depending on their perceived value to the investor, so it is, therefore, possible to make a capital loss or gain on a fixed interest holding. As a rule of thumb, when interest rates are low, they are considered to be more valuable, and when interest rates are high, they are seen to be less valuable. For example, if a gilt or corporate bond has a coupon of 3% and a savings account is paying just 1% elsewhere, there is value in holding the bond or gilt and its value will rise; however, if savings accounts are paying 4% elsewhere, the 3% will have no value to the investor and so that will be reflected in the capital price. That's a very simplistic explanation of how they work, although there are many other factors that affect their value. The returns that an investor can receive are in the form of either income from interest or an increase in the capital value of the bond when there is demand.

They are always found in more cautious investment portfolios as they do not fluctuate in value in the same way that shares tend to. They are, in fact, a very important part of a portfolio and they will support shorter-term income needs. Money that will need to be accessed within three to seven years for either income or capital needs should be invested into fixed interest investments.

Property

The property that is held within a professional investment portfolio will not usually be residential property. It will be commercial property, such as shopping centres or big office blocks, and this is because the tenants (people renting the buildings) are usually long term and not likely to suddenly leave. This gives more certainty and stability to the fund managers that are invested in them. Most of the big shopping centres and office complexes in the UK are owned by pension funds.

The returns that you will receive from an investment in property are from the rental income, known as the rental yield, and the increase in the capital value of the property.

Property is termed a real asset and many people like to invest in it because it is tangible meaning that you can see it and touch it and walk into it, and that gives it a feeling of security. Because it is not valued constantly like the stock market is, it appears less volatile.

As I discussed earlier, it is not easy to sell property quickly and so it is not a liquid investment. If you are invested in a fund that contains property, you may not be able to cash your money in straight away if the market is bad and the fund manager is unable to sell the asset. Investing in buy to let property is also very popular; in fact, in this country, we seem to have an obsession with buying property. Property can be a useful part of a portfolio, but I believe that the mindset of property being the only asset you should invest in is a foolish one. I frequently hear a 'you can't lose' attitude from people who are really pro property, but I am afraid that I do not agree. It is very difficult to do any sort of tax planning when money is in property - income tax, capital gains tax and inheritance tax all need to be considered, along with stamp duty. There are also ongoing maintenance costs to consider as well as managing tenants if you hold the property yourself. Property can, in fact, be a very costly investment to hold. Yes, you can get an agent to manage the property but this eats into your profits. In a depressed market, it can be almost impossible to sell a property. My advice with property is to proceed with caution and definitely don't put all of your eggs in one basket.

Shares

By owning a share, you have ownership of a small part of that company. If you hold that share directly, you could decide to go to their annual general meetings and cast votes. Although I am sure that you can think of things that you would much rather do!

The valuation of a share is a very complex calculation to understand and I will spare you the pain of explaining it to you! Broadly, it depends on the value of the company's assets and liabilities, its profits and cash flow, its ability to pay dividends to shareholders, service its debts and the stock market perception of how that company will perform in the future.

Some company's shares can be hugely overvalued because they are the 'in thing' to invest in, think Facebook shares; and some company's shares can be hugely undervalued because the market has decided that they don't like them, think bank shares. This is known as market sentiment and can mean that the value of a share can vary wildly in a single day. A company can lose most of its value in one day if there is some bad news and the market doesn't like it.

A good fund manager will understand all of this and invest in shares based on the information they have about a company, current and future economic trends and cycles and not what is in fashion.

The return that you get from a share comes in the form of dividends and in the increase in capital value of the share. A dividend is a share of the profits of the company and is usually paid half yearly. When a company is doing well and making a profit, it will declare a dividend to share those profits with its shareholders. If the company is not doing so well, they will hold the profits back to boost the company.

As an investment and part of a portfolio, shares are very important, and as the economy grows and prices increase, so will, generally, the value of shares. For this reason they can protect your money from the effects of inflation and offer real returns. However, there are times when markets can really struggle as they have over the last ten years. When times are like these, clever fund managers and good asset allocation are vital. I will explain asset allocation to you in just a moment. Shares are an incredibly important part of a portfolio as they are a real asset and will give your portfolio the real growth that it needs over time. They are not suitable for short term investment though and should only be thought of as part of your long term investment strategy. History shows that the longest that it has taken the market to recover losses was seven years and so this should be borne in mind when using them in a portfolio.

Other investments

The following are not defined as true asset classes but can be found in an investment portfolio that is higher on the risk scale.

Commodities

This includes all sorts of things such as oil, gas, grain, cotton, energy and metal to name a few. They tend to fall into the higher risk end of investments because they can be very volatile. However, depending on your risk profile, you may have a fund that includes commodities.

Gold

This has been a popular investment through the financial crisis because it behaves very differently to the traditional asset classes. The technical term for this is uncorrelated. The rise and fall of the stock markets and property market have no effect on gold at all. It has been seen as a safe haven to invest throughout the financial crisis and its value has increased significantly. Likewise, your gold jewellery will have increased in value. As part of an investment portfolio it provides what is known as a hedge against the effects of inflation, which means that it reduces the risk.

The importance of diversification and asset allocation

Diversification

In an investment portfolio it is so important to spread your risk and not have all of your eggs in one basket.

To give you an example; if you had all of your money in Burberry shares when they issued a profit warning, you would have lost

20% of the value of your investment instantly. However, if you had some Burberry shares, some Apple shares, some Taylor Wimpey shares, some Lloyds Banking Group shares, some mining shares, some government gilts, some property and some Gold, you would have a portfolio that was diversified as the shares are all in different sectors. In this example, you would have shares in retail, technology, construction, banking and mining, as well as some fixed interest with your gilts, some property and some gold. This would mean that if shares in one sector or company were doing badly, the shares in another sector or company could be doing well, therefore balancing your risk; this is the meaning of diversification.

As well as spreading the risk across different sectors, the risk will also be spread across different countries and economies.

Asset allocation

The Wikipedia definition of asset allocation is as follows:
Asset allocation is an investment strategy that attempts to balance risk versus reward by adjusting the percentage of each asset in an investment portfolio according to the investors risk tolerance, goals and investment time frame.

The principle behind asset allocation is that different assets perform differently in different economic conditions. By having the right spread of assets in your portfolio, it is, in theory, possible to reduce the amount of risk and volatility that you are exposed to. Research suggests that correct asset allocation reduces portfolio volatility by more than 90%.

Correct allocation will maximise the returns and minimise the risk. The theory is that an investor does not need to take an excessive amount of risk to achieve the desired returns.

There are two types of asset allocation, which are known as strategic and tactical asset allocation.

Strategic asset allocation looks at the correct mix of assets for the long term objectives of the portfolio. For example, for your risk profile you may have a strategic asset allocation of 10% cash, 25% fixed interest, 5% property, 30% UK equities, 20% European equities and 10% north American equities. This forms the benchmark of your portfolio.

Tactical asset allocation allows the fund manager to make tactical decisions within that strategic benchmark to take advantage of opportunities that present themselves in the market due to current themes and economic factors. You need a good fund manager to do this and get it right, and so the research adopted by your financial adviser is very important.

The portfolio needs to be rebalanced on a regular basis to ensure that the asset allocation remains correct, as due to the natural fluctuations of different funds and assets classes, your portfolio will become unbalanced over time. Your portfolio needs to be reviewed annually as a minimum and, in some cases, six monthly or even quarterly.

Are you still with me?! It's a lot to take in but so important to understand. Leaving all of your money in cash is going to kill its value with the effects of inflation, and so the only way to try and combat this and make some real returns is to invest. The more of an understanding you have of the basics, the less scary it will hopefully feel to you. It is so important that you have your money spread across the right assets and investments for your income and capital needs, your capacity for loss and your tolerance for risk. Your relationship with your adviser is vital and a good adviser will explain it all to you and ensure that you feel comfortable with the investments that you make.

CHAPTER 11

Keeping the tax man happy

I can already feel your eyes glazing over at the thought of having to read a chapter about tax! Yes, I know it's not the most knicker-gripping of subjects, but it is really important to have a basic understanding of it, mainly so you don't have HMRC (The Taxman) breathing down your neck!

Not understanding the tax implications of assets in a divorce can really catch you out, so you need to have some awareness of what it is. Tax will impact your ongoing lifestyle and needs to be taken account of when planning for your future.

When it comes to dealing with the taxman, the first thing you need is a good accountant. My accountant is fantastic, she knows her stuff, is down to earth and I can ask her anything. She sorts out all of my receipts and returns and takes the pain away. Find yourself a nice lady accountant who you like and who will get the job done for you.

A brief introduction to tax

What is tax?

Tax is a financial levy imposed by the government to ensure that we contribute to the state on income that we earn or gains we make from our investments. Failure to pay these charges is punishable by law.

Why do I have to pay it?

We are all required to make a contribution to the state from our earnings or gains, and if we don't, we could be fined or even go to prison.

When do I have to pay it?

Each year you will have to submit a tax return to HMRC (Her Majesty's Revenue & Customs, otherwise known as the taxman!). If you do this on paper, it has to be returned by 31st October following the end of the tax year, and if submitting online, it needs to be done by the 31st January following the end of the tax year. You will also need to pay any tax due at the same time.

The tax year runs from the 6th April to the following 5th April. If you were submitting your tax return online for the tax year ending 5th April 2013, you would need to do it by 31st January 2014.

If your tax return is late, you will get fined £100 plus £10 per day for every day that you are late with your return up to 90 days, and then you get another £300 or 5% of the tax you owe on top of that after 6 months with the same again after 12 months. The fines are very hefty and so you need to ensure that your returns are filed on time.

Income tax

The first of the main taxes that I will explain is income tax. It is the most common and regular tax that you are likely to pay. You will pay income tax on all income that you receive, whether you have earned it by working, or not. Some examples of income that you will pay tax on are employed earnings, self employed earnings, interest on your savings accounts, rental income from investment properties, dividend income from shares, income received from a trust or income you receive from your husband's company. You will have to pay tax on income that you receive from anywhere in the world.

How much tax will you have to pay on your income?

Everyone is allowed to have some income without having to pay any tax and this is known as your personal allowance. For the tax year 2013/14, this is £9,440. If your income is coming from savings accounts and investments only, the next £2,790 of your income is taxed at 10% as long as your total income is not more than £12,230. If it is more than this, the next £32,010 of your income is taxed at 20%, known as basic rate tax. The next portion of your income up to £150,000 is taxed at 40%, which is known as higher rate tax, and anything over and above that is taxed at 45%, known as additional rate tax.

Dividends are taxed differently, just to confuse matters! Basic rate tax on dividends is 10% and is already taken before you receive the dividend so you don't have to pay it again. Higher rate dividend tax is 32.5% meaning you have to pay another

25% on the dividend you receive and additional rate tax is 42.5% meaning that you have to pay an additional 36.1% on the amount that you receive. God knows who came up with such daft rates of tax for dividends!

Maintenance payments that you receive from your husband will already have been taxed as his income, so you won't have to pay tax on these.

If you have been given rental property, a large amount of cash or investments as part of the settlement, you will have income tax to pay and need to send a tax return each year.

There are certain ways of reducing your income tax liability, such as making pension contributions and charitable donations. Your financial adviser can help you with this.

Capital gains tax

This is a tax that is paid when you make a profit on an asset that you have sold or transferred. This could be an investment property, a share portfolio, jewellery, a painting, overseas investments and trust investments. Again, the tax is payable on your worldwide assets. So, if you have a property overseas and you sell it for a profit, it's likely that you will have to pay some tax on the gain. The only property asset that is exempt (subject to certain rules) is the house that you live in, known as your principle private residence.

Married couples can transfer assets to each other without having to pay any tax, but if you made a gift to your children of, say, an investment property that had gone up in value since you bought it, there would be tax to pay on that gain.

Once you separate from your husband, you have until the end of the tax year to make any transfers before you end up having to pay capital gains on assets that he passes to you as part of the divorce. So, for example, if he is giving you an investment property or a share portfolio that has gone up in value since he bought it and he gives it to you more than a year after you have separated, he will have to pay tax on the gain. Capital gains tax can have a significant impact on assets transferred as part of the divorce settlement and timing is key, you should seek advice from a tax adviser before you agree on a settlement.

How much will you have to pay?

Capital gains tax can be complicated but I am going to give you a really simple explanation as to how it works. You start with the sale price of the asset, which was, for example, £100,000, then deduct the original cost, which was, for example, £70,000, and then also any costs involved in buying it, selling it and improving it, so let's assume this was £10,000. You now are left with a gain of £20,000. You have an amount each year that you can have in gains without paying any tax and this is known as the annual exemption. For the tax year 2013/14, this is £10,900. So that leaves you with a taxable gain of £9,100 and this is added to your income to decide which rate of tax you have to pay. If you are a basic rate taxpayer, as described in the income tax section, you pay 18% tax on that gain, and if you are a higher rate taxpayer, you will pay 28% tax on the gain.

That's the dead simple way of calculating capital gains tax.

This will also need to go onto your annual tax return and your accountant will be able to help you.

Inheritance Tax

This is also known as death duty! Its correct terminology is a tax imposed on the privilege of receiving property by inheritance or legal succession and assessed on the value of the property received, which can be in lifetime or death. It is a very complex tax, but I would like to give you a brief overview so that you have an understanding of what it is.

Example:

Jenny's parents are married and they have a house worth £1 million and cash, investments and other assets worth another £500,000. Jenny's dad has passed away and left everything to her mum.

On the death of Jenny's mother she leaves everything to Jenny as the sole beneficiary. She made no other gifts in her lifetime and neither did Jenny's father.

There is a certain amount of money that can be passed without having to pay any tax and this is known as the nil rate band. It is called nil rate because the tax rate is 0%. Each person has their own nil rate band and it is currently (2013/14) £325,000 with anything over that being taxed at 40%. Married couples who leave everything to each other also pass their own nil rate band across to each other.

Going back to our example regarding Jenny's father's death, the £325,000 nil rate band passed to her Mother, so that on her death, £650,000 of inheritance could be passed onto Jenny without paying any tax on it; the rest is taxed at 40%.

So, Jenny's parents left her with £1.5 million, she could inherit £650,000 tax-free and then the rest is taxed at 40%; therefore, in this example, Jenny would have to pay tax of £340,000.

It's a huge chunk of your inheritance and would come as a big shock if you weren't aware that it was going to be charged.

The same will be true of any money that you pass to your children. You will only have one nil rate band of £325,000 to pass to them because you have been divorced, and if you remarry someone that has their own children, this can add a whole other layer of complication to things.

This is a very simple calculation of inheritance tax to you show you how big a tax bill it is. It is, however, much more complex than that, and if you are making large transfers into trust for your children in later years, you will need advice from someone specialising in inheritance tax, which will be either a lawyer or financial adviser or both, depending on what you are putting in the trust.

Inheritance tax can be avoided, at least in part, by proper financial planning and ensuring that money that will not be needed in lifetime is gifted away in the right way. Once a gift is made, the person making it will have to survive seven years to ensure that there is no tax to pay. For example, your parents could make a gift to you either directly or into a trust. If they then survive for seven years after making that gift, it is said to be outside of their estate, which basically means that they don't own it any more as far as the taxman is concerned and there is no tax to pay on it.

I have explained this to you in a very simplistic way but as you can see it's pretty complicated stuff and it's absolutely vital that you get advice from a properly trained financial planner who understands the complexities and can help you do things in the right way.

The best way to approach matters of taxation is to get advice. I have given you very simplistic overviews of each of the main areas of taxation, but they are all complex as more and more layers of law affect them. It is possible to reduce your tax liability in all areas with the correct financial planning. However, you must seek advice before a transaction takes place, before the end of an accounting year or the end of the tax year, as if you do not plan beforehand, the opportunity may be lost.

CHAPTER 12

In conclusion

As little girls we are taught that it is rude to talk about money. We are conditioned from a young age to not discuss money or finances and that it is not a woman's job. However, since then, the world has changed dramatically and in more and more households, the woman is the breadwinner or the sole earner. The problem is, though, that we are not always well equipped emotionally to deal with it and many women lack confidence around money, even those of us who are in charge of the purse strings and are used to dealing with the money. I have had to really look at my own relationship with money and it has been enlightening. It has also allowed me to have far greater empathy with others. I have learned that understanding your relationship with money and healing issues around money and self worth is the first step to attracting more wealth into your life.

With around 45% of marriages now ending in divorce, more and more women are finding themselves in charge of the finances. To have to deal with the emotional upheaval of divorce and then make strategic decisions around money when you are not used to dealing with the finances is hugely stressful. Even those of us who are used to looking after the family finances will find it a huge strain on top of all of the emotional pain. It is so important to think strategically about money, it must be a business transaction that takes account of your long term needs and not just a short term view. I really believe that it is incredibly important that you have a divorce coach to help you come to terms with your emotions before you start to make decisions about the finances. Financial decisions made in an emotional state are never going to be good ones and could affect your financial security forever. Don't be tempted to make fast decisions for the sake of getting it over and done with or because you are being pressurised. Likewise, don't try and punish your husband for emotional hurt financially or via solicitors, it won't get you anywhere and it will just end up costing you a lot of money, which is money that you both could have had. Take your time to work on your emotions first and then deal with the finances; you will be glad you did.

Use the right professionals for the right job. Your lawyer will be a very expensive divorce coach. Pay for good financial advice and use a private investigator if you need to.

Getting a really crystal clear picture of your outgoings is the most important step that you can take in gaining control of your finances. True financial planning hinges on a thorough understanding of your spending plans, both now and in the future, and getting it right from the outset will save you a lot of stress in the future. Get in the habit of putting 10% of all your income into a savings account that you don't ever touch. This is first step in improving your relationship with money and you will be amazed at the way that wealth finds its way to you once you start to do this. I have read many books on the subject of money and our relationship with it and I have provided an index of recommended reading for you, both on the money front and also to help you with the emotional side.

Get yourself a good financial planner. Someone who takes time to understand you, your goals and objectives and what your fears and worries are. They should be someone who will guide you through the process one step at a time. A good financial planner is not someone who just takes your divorce settlement and shoves it in an investment and then does a mandatory annual review but nothing else. A great financial planner builds a relationship with you and takes time to explain everything so that you feel confident and secure. They will build you a roadmap of the future and help you along that path. Once you have found this person, financial planning and investing becomes far less scary and stressful.

Make sure that you cut all financial ties as quickly as you can. Don't be tempted to hang on to joint accounts or debts because of a misguided emotional attachment; it won't serve you either financially or emotionally.

Please don't hang on to assets because of an emotional attachment, it can prove to be such a huge financial mistake. It's tempting to hang onto a house for the sake of the children, but children adapt to new situations quickly and moving into a new house can be an adventure for them. Having a fresh start in a new house will help you to move on far more quickly than being stuck in the same house with all the memories of the past.

Spend and invest wisely; remember that the settlement that you agree has to potentially last you for the rest of your life, unless you have earnings in your own right. Don't be tempted to go on huge spending sprees to make yourself feel better, it won't.

Stick to your budget when buying a property and don't invest in fad investments. Remember, do the opposite to the crowd!

If you require access to any of the professionals that I have mentioned in the book, please do get in touch. You can find me by visiting my website www.hannahfoxley.com or via a Google search.

I hope that you have found this book useful and that you are able to dip in and out and reference it whenever you need some help with the finances. I very much enjoyed writing it for you. I wish you the very best of luck with your new life and your newfound financial freedom.

Hannah

RECOMMENDED READING

The Naked Divorce	Adele Theron
How to make a hell of a profit and still go to heaven	John Demartini
Financial Recovery	Karen McCall
The Energy of Money	Maria Nemeth
The Gifts of Imperfection	Brene Brown
Think and Grow Rich	Napoleon Hill
Attract Money Now	Joe Vitale
The Emotion behind Money	Julie Murphy Casserly
Divorce and Splitting Up	Marilyn Stow
Become a Money Magnet	Marie-Claire Carlyle

AUTHOR BIO

Hannah Foxley is a Chartered Financial Planner and a Fellow of The Personal Finance Society and has been advising clients since 2003.

She is passionate about helping women who are facing divorce to better understand the finances. Taking the fear and worry away, she leaves them feeling confident and secure.

Two times breast cancer survivor, Hannah knows a thing or two about the curve balls life can throw at you. She is now a speaker and inspirer of other women. Through her talks and blogs, she shares how she took a life threatening illness and used it as a catalyst to turn her life around, starting her business just three weeks after finishing cancer treatment. Having faced life's challenges, she is able to communicate with her clients with great empathy and understanding.

Hannah's passion now extends to doing extensive charity work, where she pledges to give 5% of her book profits to cancer charities and is a proud ambassador for both Breakthrough Breast Cancer and Breast Cancer Campaign.

She is a regular contributor to many articles and blogs on finance for women and has appeared on Sky News as a finance expert.

www.hannahfoxley.com
Twitter: @hannah_foxley
Linked in: uk.linkedin.com/in/hannahfoxley
Google +: https://plus.google.
com/u/0/112308275604339458309/posts
Facebook: https://www.facebook.com/TheWealthyDivorcee

TESTIMONIALS

"I had already divorced when I read this book. I wish it had been available before. Going through a divorce is the most difficult and mind-blowing situation I have been in. This book would have saved my children and I time, money and heartache. The most poignant chapter is the one that describes leaving the marital home, which was for me the hardest part of the whole proceeding. If I had read this book first it would have saved me nearly having a nervous breakdown. Great work Hannah you are an amazing person for getting this book so right."

– Suzanne Nyman

"A fantastic practical guide to financial survival post or pre divorce. Hannah imparts tips and advice in a warm and easy to digest format. A must read for any female facing divorce who wants to get herself back on to her own two feet quickly and effectively."

– Vanessa Vallely
CEO, Founder WeAreTheCity.com

"Excellent reference book, easy to follow and makes for a great source of knowledge. An accurate and useful guide for those going through a divorce. Highly recommended."

– Camilla Choudhury - Khawaja LL.B Hons LL.M
Barrister/Lecturer in Law
www.thewomenslawyer.co.uk

"Hannah Foxley's book is just what I needed to get myself ready for my new life of financial independence. Despite having been divorced for a full year, I had fallen into inertia over my finances and I needed help to move on. This book shows that actually it isn't too late to get your finances in order even after you're on your own. The book's no-nonsense approach is just the right combination of professional expertise, personal experience, empathy and warmth. It's never too late to learn and change and thanks to The Wealthy Divorcee I feel well equipped to face my financial future."

– Jane Gizbert

9201445R00107

Printed in Great Britain
by Amazon.co.uk, Ltd.,
Marston Gate.